CW00455636

IN SEARCH OF THE SACRED

JOSEF PIEPER

In Search of the Sacred

Contributions to an Answer

Translated by
Lothar Krauth

IGNATIUS PRESS   SAN FRANCISCO

Originally published in German as
Was Heisst "Sakral"?
© 1988 Schwabenverlag AG
Ostfildern bei Stuttgart

Cover design by Roxanne Mei Lum
Cover border by Pamela Kennedy
Calligraphy by Victoria Hoke Lane

With ecclesiastical approval
© 1991 Ignatius Press, San Francisco
All rights reserved
ISBN 0–89870–301–8
Library of Congress catalogue number 90–81770
Printed in the United States of America

CONTENTS

CHAPTER ONE

THE SACRED AND ITS NEGATION

An Initial Approach

WHAT DO WE mean by "sacred"? As always, the answer ought to begin with a direct look at some tangible, practical situations, identifying the phenomenon, gathering what can be observed.

We are in Frankfurt in West Germany in May 1948. For the centennial celebration of the National Assembly the Pauluskirche (St. Paul's Church, seat of the first Assembly) had been restored, while the city all around still lay in ruins. The newly founded Association of German Authors, too, held an assembly in that classical rotunda of red sandstone. The participants, leaving a resplendent midmorning outside, came strolling in, conversing with each other and mildly curious. Quite a few of them continued to smoke their cigarettes, unabashed, and others lit theirs. But then came the announcement, "No smoking, please! You are in a church." My neighbor looked up in surprise: How come this is a church? I had to agree with him; the architecture alone, at any

Keynote address for the Annual Meeting of the Goerres Society, Oct. 9, 1969, at the courthouse in Münster. Printed in *Hochland* 61 (1969) and published by Verlag der Arche (Zurich, 1970).

rate, would *not* be a sufficient indication. My neighbor paused, then remarked, "Even though it was a church, I mean, a real church—why in the world no smoking?"

A year later, in Berlin-Treptow. Once again an emphasis on "no smoking!"—this time while entering the huge memorial park for the fallen heroes of the Red army.

And recently I had the same experience in Israel, in the dining room of my hotel. The American guests at the next table, after their meal, readied their cigarettes when came the discreet but firm request, "No smoking, please!" But why not? Here, indeed, not because of the place, rather because of the time: Friday evening, the beginning of the Sabbath.

Clearly, in all these situations any consideration of possible disturbance or interference, as for instance in a lecture hall or a surgery room, does not apply, much less the thought of fire danger, as in an airplane during takeoff and landing. Nor does this no-smoking rule here imply any general contempt for smoking as though it were something indecent. No, it becomes evident rather that some kind of demarcation is involved and applied here, a borderline separating a special place and an exceptional span of time from just any common and ordinary place and time. The nonsmoking rule, incidentally, appears to be quite an appropriate example indeed. Bertold Brecht once remarked: "I declare that a single man in the audience at a Shakespeare performance, smoking a cigar, could well precipitate the demise of Western art."[1]

Those who step over the threshold to enter that "other" realm are expected to comport themselves differently from what would otherwise be common. Whoever enters a mosque or the walled-in precinct of an Indian temple takes off his shoes. The line of separation, in the latter instance, may perchance be drawn so rigorously that, as a non-Hindu, you are not admitted to the innermost sanctuary at all. Men in Christian churches remove their hats; the same happens at an open grave, but also during the national anthem. A Jew, in contrast, covers his head, not only in the synagogue but also whenever he prays. In Tiberias, as I stepped into the enclosure surrounding Moses Maimonides' tomb, the custodian hurried toward me with alarm in his gestures: my head was not covered!

A place of worship usually demands silence; at any rate, uncontrolled shouting and laughter

[1] Brecht, *Gesammelte Werke,* vol. 15 (Frankfurt, 1963–64), 77.

are frowned upon. At the entrance to St. Mark's Cathedral in Venice, tourists who are clad too scantily are turned back. In such places, the paraphernalia of public curiosity as well are usually eyed with suspicion. In many Christian churches, at least during services, taking pictures is not allowed; the same is true in the temples of orthodox Hinduism. The Pueblo Indians of New Mexico even resent any camera-equipped visitor who dares so much as to approach the entrance of their underground ceremonial chamber.

Should the stranger, the outsider, the uninitiated inquire as to the meaning of these rules of conduct, which may appear to him unreasonable and often quite cumbersome, he would be given answers that in spite of all variety in specific instances always agree on this: the reason is to show reverence and respect. Respect for what? For something that at any rate requires and deserves homage and reverence. Should he persist in asking what concrete and specific reality there be that deserves such reverence, then, presumably, the answers would no longer converge. But they would still unanimously inform the questioner about something that is (or should be) "sacred" to man, be it specified as the "majesty of death", the dignity of the fatherland, the honor of fallen heroes, or directly as the tangible presence of something divine, if not of God himself.

All such answers would indeed flow from the common basic conviction that within the world's total framework of space and time, accessible to man, there do exist specific exceptional and separated spaces and times, distinct from the ordinary, and therefore possessing a special and unique dignity.

Such circumscription of something that eminently deserves reverence is also clearly intended in the original meaning of the related vocabulary. Even a merely superficial consultation of appropriate dictionaries will show this. *Hagios,* for example, the Greek term for "holy", implies its opposite, *koinōs* (average, common, ordinary). And the precinct dedicated to the gods, containing temple or altar, is called *témenos,* meaning "carved out" from the common public domain. The Latin verb *sancire,* the root of *sanctus* (holy, sacred), also means "to fence off, to circumscribe". "The ancient Roman originally used *sanctio* to indicate the boundaries of a sacred space and its protection against infringement and profanation."[2] Regarding contemporary speech, the findings are not much different. *Sacré* is something that belongs to an *ordre des choses sépare*[3] (to a category of things set apart). And the Oxford Dictionary lists under *sacred* also the meaning *set apart*. More complicated, however, and less transparent is the German language in this respect. Several terms offer their services at once: *heilig, geweiht, sakral* (holy, consecrated, sacred). Moreover, these terms do not each carry a precise meaning, not even in philosophical contexts. Immanuel Kant, for example, formally defining the concept of "holiness", intends to understand it as "the perfect conformity of the will to the moral law",[4] which at first sounds quite precise. Yet a few lines further down he calls the moral law itself "holy", clearly disagreeing with his own definition. It appears that here an entirely different meaning of the term *holy* comes to the fore. This other meaning, not different from the corresponding Greek and Latin expressions, indeed denotes that specific dignity that stands out in the daily flow of an indifferent reality, which interrupts the routine and explicitly

---

[3] A. Lalande, *Vocabulaire technique et critique de la Philosophie* (Paris, 1962), 937.
[4] I. Kant, *Kritik der praktischen Vernunft,* ed. K. Vorländer (Leipzig, 1920), 156.

sets itself apart from the ordinary—a dignity entitled to special forms of respect on the part of
man.

To repeat, then: wherever something is deemed
"sacred" in this sense, there the preceding fundamental conviction obtains that the world is not
simply homogeneous, that neither space nor time
is such. Mircea Eliade,[5] interpreting the nature
of the sacred, is perfectly correct in this respect,
however questionable his total conception may
be. A sacred space is "different" from all other
locations. And if Easter and Christmas, if the
Sabbath and Sunday, are taken as periods of "sacred" times, then it is declared that they are not
"just like any other day". This, of course, provides only negative information. The question
remains as to what constitutes the special and
separated character of the sacred and in what positive reality the sacred itself consists.

Those who decide to face such questions nowadays will find themselves immediately on the bat-
tlefield of a heated public discussion, not at all
within the lofty confines of academe. The term
desacralization is indeed no longer used simply to
describe in objective terms a contemporary social

[5] M. Eliade, *Das Heilige und das Profane* (Hamburg, 1957),
13, 40.

development, admittedly rampant and pervasive. No, it has become the catchword for a program pursuing a specific goal, lately employing even "theological" arguments. Thus we are told that Christ has sanctified the totality of the world, and therefore *everything* is sacred. Others insist that he has in fact so liberated the world and all of humanity as to restore to them their true worldly and secular identity.[6] It has been proclaimed outright that "we Christians are no longer able or allowed to acknowledge anything as sacred."[7] If this were true, if indeed—for whatever reason—everything were indiscriminately "sacred" or indiscriminately "profane", then any distinction between sacred and profane would in fact be meaningless and without justification.

The term *profane,* incidentally, I have so far avoided on purpose. Its original meaning, as I see it, does not contain any hint of impropriety, for it indicated nothing else than the area in front of the temple (*fanum*), in front of its gates, "outside". But, of course, our latter use of this term has changed the original meaning considerably.

---

[6] See Eduard Syndicus, "Entsakralisierung. Ein Literaturbericht", *Theologie und Philosophie* 42 (1967): 577.

[7] See Herbert Kuhn, "Tun, was Jesus getan hat", *Deutsches Allgemeines Sonntagsblatt,* Dec. 12, 1967, p. 3.

It is not of much help, therefore, when Roger Caillois evasively—though in strictly formal terms still correctly—states that the "sacred", *le sacré,* could only be defined in contrast to the "profane".[8] It has to be explained, right there, what *content* is given to the concepts of both "sacred" and "profane".

Analogies

I am not yet prepared to give such an explanation, since first I wish to offer for your consideration, all too summarily perhaps, two analogous distinctions that nowadays are also systematically questioned and attacked. I am referring to the distinctions between poetry and nonpoetry and between philosophy and science.

Concerning the first of these distinctions, we see for example Bertold Brecht's "non-Aristotelian poetics"—which he himself, fortunately, never followed—as ultimately aiming at the annihilation of all poetry. The effect of great poetry, the catharsis triggered through the awareness of deeper existential dimensions, is denounced as es-

[8] R. Caillois, *L'homme et le sacré,* 3rd ed. (Paris, 1950), 11.

capism, a flight into illusion. The spectator, says Brecht, has to keep "his cigar lit" and himself critically alert for the political action that will transform the world. According to this opinion, there is nothing to be acknowledged except the prose of class struggle from which nobody may be excused, not even for one hour. Such "prose", of course, explicitly "nonpoetic", can sail under many different flags: five-year plan, entertainment, sensationalism, psychological empiricism, and so on.

To this corresponds, in the area of the theory of science, the negation of philosophy, which incidentally flows from a similar mentality. To engage in philosophy, meaning to contemplate the totality of reality and existence in view of ultimate reasons; to confront the human mind, by nature oriented toward the universe of all that is, with its true though unfathomable object—all this, we are told, is meaningless. The only authentic cognitive approach to reality would rather be that of the empirical sciences, legitimated through verifiable results. All human search for knowledge, in the words of the young Rudolf Carnap, would in fact be nothing else but "physics."[9]

---

[9] See also the manifesto of the "Wiener Kreis", *Wissenschaftliche Weltauffassung* (Vienna, 1929).

Such pronouncements do not, as a rule, come out of the blue; more likely than not are they rather reactions to a devious self-understanding on the part of poetry and philosophy themselves. Considering, for instance, the illusory idealization of man and society, deemed "poetic" by the Schiller epigones, we may find the reaction of all those "naturalisms" and "verisms", and Bertold Brecht's reaction as well, more than understandable. And the insistence on experience as the root of all human knowledge is, of course, entirely justified in view of a philosophy that fancifully defines itself as "comprehension of the absolute" (Hegel)[10] or as "anticipation of all possible experience" (Fichte).[11]

Lately we have witnessed the attempt to provide new definitions for poetry and philosophy and thus to salvage their autonomy. Philosophy, for example, is declared essentially distinct from science because it does not deal with reality at all but exclusively with the language used by science to talk about reality. And Jean-Paul Sartre[12] pro-

---

[10] *Briefe von und an Hegel,* ed. Johannes Hoffmeister (Hamburg, 1953), 2:216.

[11] *Erste Einleitung in die Wissenschaftslehre,* ed. Fritz Medicus (Leipzig, 1944), 31.

[12] J.-P. Sartre, *Was ist Literatur?* (Hamburg, 1958), 11ff.

poses to consider the everyday "prosaic" language, including that of a "writer", as the use of words for a specific purpose, while we should acknowledge as a poet anybody who indeed refuses to *use* words and make them serve his own purposes, who rather deals with words as having purpose and reason in and by themselves. Such an interpretation, it seems to me, fails to do justice to the nature of poetry as well as of prose.

In all this I see analogies to the interpretation of "holy" (sacred) and "profane". Everything comes out wrong as soon as it is overlooked or denied that poetry and prose are but two different modes of speaking about what is real, and that philosophy no less than science attempts to know and understand the vast subject matter called "reality". Just so do we miss the real point, by necessity, if we fail to see the contrast of "sacred" versus "profane" equally *within* one common and comprehensive reality. If it were really true, for example, that the sacred and the profane (as some questionable interpretation of the "mythical-archaic" world view asserts) would confront each other like "two radically heterogeneous worlds" (E. Durkheim),[13] like "cosmos" and "chaos", like

[13] Lalande, *Vocabulaire*, 937.

"reality" and "fiction" (or "pseudoreality"), separated from each other by an "abyss" (M. Eliade);[14]
if there were really no *solidarité du sacré et du profane*
(common ground between the sacred and the profane) whatsoever (J.-P. Audet);[15] if, in other
words, the world "outside" the temple gates could
by no means claim to be created "good" and to
be in a certain sense "sacred" itself; if that absurd
and simplistic claim[16] were right that the existence
of any "sacred" space would imply total license
"to do *outside* whatever you want"—if all this
were the case, then a Christian would indeed have
to reject the distinction between sacred and profane as unacceptable.

And if now, as we are told in addition to and
on top of all this, anything "sacred" were to be
marked essentially by the remote air of its pomp
and circumstances, by hierarchical rigidity, by
an outlandish ritual, and so on—then the demand
for "desacralization" would become quite understandable and indeed inevitable. This, then, would
attack and deny not only all pseudosacredness,

[14] Eliade, *Das Heilige und das Profane,* 10, 13, 18.

[15] J.-P. Audet, "Le sacré et le profane", *Nouvelle Revue
Théologique* 79 (1957).

[16] See Herbert Kuhn, "Tun, was Jesus getan hat", 3.

the original target, but also the entire realm covered by the term *sacred,* including what legitimately and authentically is called such.

The question, of course, remains: What is "authentically" sacred?

"Sacred" Does Not Apply to God

One aspect has to be clarified right away; otherwise, all further considerations will remain hopelessly ambiguous. Whoever uses the term *holy* as we do here, in contrast to *profane,* can only mean a quality pertaining to something of this our world and by no means describing the inner nature of God himself. In this respect the Latin— and Latin-derived—usage of the term is much more precise than ours. Although God, of course, and God alone, is in the ultimate and deepest sense "holy", we never apply to him the terms *sacer, sacré, sakral* (sacred)—which fact already clarifies a further point: whatever is not sacred cannot be conceived as "Godless" by definition, much less as opposed to God. The terms *holy* and *sacred,* therefore, are used here neither for the infinite perfection of God nor for the spiritual superiority of a man; rather, they are used to mean certain tangible things, spaces, times, and actions as possessing the specific quality of being separated from the ordinary and directed toward the realm of the divine. Incidentally, a man, too, could be called "holy" in this specific sense; but then, once again, not his moral perfection, though really beyond doubt, would thus be indicated, but rather his special orientation toward the divine realm, his "consecration" and "sanctification".

From such nonordinary orientation toward a realm beyond the merely human, from such "intensified" divine presence, which is not encountered in all places or at all times, there derives directly also the *boundary* separating and dividing what is "holy" in this sense from what is "profane". The term *profane* here indeed denotes the area of what is common and devoid of that special distinction as mentioned; not at all does *profane* necessarily mean *unholy*—though there surely exist realities that are explicitly unholy and thus may represent the extremes of profanity. There is, of course, some justification in declaring, say, that *all* bread is "sacred" (because created by God, and life giving, and so forth); or that *every* parcel of soil is "sacred ground"—yes, one is justified to speak in this manner since it does not imply the denial that there may be also and nevertheless a bread uniquely "sacred" and a precinct singularly "consecrated".

Here we can already identify certain preconditions that must obtain before any sense at all for the sacred may be expected, any sense indeed for what it implies: that something by its very nature is set apart from the commonplace of everyday life. These preconditions are obviously not satisfied whenever the existence of a divine and supernatural realm is simply denied. And further, should the notion be rejected of an "intensified" divine presence above the ordinary, connected to specific places, times, persons, or actions and therefore "datable", in Karl Barth's words, then this, too, would bespeak blindness for the phenomenon we are discussing here. I suspect that such blindness, hard to cure, is involved whenever "desacralization" becomes a program and a battle cry, no matter what arguments are advanced.

But at this point, discussing the sacred, we still have to deal first with the phenomenon itself.

Actio Sacra (Sacred Action)

We commonly use the expressions "sacred place", "sacred time", "sacred action", "sacred symbol", and others like them. The new *Ordo Missae,* probably displeasing certain people, even speaks of "sacred" vessels and vestments (*de vasis sacris, de sacris vestibus;* the official rendering in the German missal as *liturgische Gefässe, liturgische Kleidung* [liturgical vessels, liturgical vestments] is, mildly put, imprecise). We have to ask here whether the "sacred" instances listed in this decidedly incomplete list should all be considered of equal importance. Or are we dealing here with primary and secondary realities, things original and things derived? The latter, I submit, is the case. More specifically: within the realm of the sacred, the "sacred *action*" can evidently claim precedence and a higher importance. This already finds its expression in the traditional statement, "Something is called sacred, *sacrum,* because of its relation to the act of public worship, *ad cultum divinum*"[17]—a statement confirmed by ethnology and philosophy of religion and no less by the theological interpretation of the Old and the New Testaments.[18]

If there exists at all a particular presence of the divine within the world of human life and history, it occurs—according to this teaching— more intensively in the "sacred action". And only in relation to such action are persons, places,

---

[17] Thomas Aquinas, *Summa theologica* 2, 2, 99, 1.

[18] See G. Kittel, *Theologisches Wörterbuch zum Neuen Testament* (Stuttgart: W. Kohlhammer, 1980), 1:106, 112.

times, and furnishings then also called "sacred".

What, then, constitutes a "sacred action"? The answer, it seems, is self-evident, say, to a Christian of African or Asian culture. We "Western" Christians, prey to the virus of desacralization, need an explicit and somewhat emphatic reminder, to wit: a "sacred action", distinct and set apart from the everyday activity and conduct by clear demarcations, is never simply "done" and "performed" but rather always "celebrated"! A "sacred action" requires "celebration". The verb *celebrare,* "from the earliest time of classical Latin up to the language of the liturgy" invariably means the same: carrying out an action, in a nonordinary manner, on the part of the community.[19] Being a social function, the "sacred action"—in contrast, for instance, to an inner act of prayer or faith or love of God—is furthermore a *physical* event, manifested in visible forms, in the audible language of call and response, in bodily movements and symbolic gestures, in proclamation and song, in the selection of vestments and vessels, and not least in communal silence. In all of this, the "doing" action of the liturgist corre-

[19] Benedicta Droste, *"Celebrare" in der römischen Liturgiesprache* (Munich, 1963), 196.

sponds to the analogous, "contemplating" coaction of the congregation.[20]

Some doubt, however, may arise especially in the mind of the more serious and thoughtful observer when attending, say, a solemn choral Mass at the monastery of Maria Laach: Could it be that these obviously impressive proceedings may in truth represent no more than an elaborate mystery play, a religious drama magnificently staged? That they remain in essence mere theatrics, empty ceremony, a "show"?

It is noteworthy that Thomas Aquinas, too, has raised a similar objection against his own position. He asks whether the dramatics of the symbolic actions could be reconciled with the "honesty" of worship—and he answers that indeed poetry and liturgy equally employ the device of expressing in concrete images what for the mind is difficult to grasp.[21]

The present-day objection, of course, aims at something totally different. It is not interested in the "meaning" of the sacred action but rather

[20] R. Guardini, "Der Kultakt und die gegenwärtige Aufgabe der Liturgie", in *Liturgie und liturgische Bildung* (Würzburg, 1966), 12.
[21] *Summa theologica* 2, 1, 101, 2 obj. 2 ad 2.

questions its substance. This objection finds it doubtful, to use a mild expression, that anything real and genuine, solid and authentic is happening in such action. It contests that something like the divine presence would in fact occur in the implementation of the sacred action. It denies, in other words, its *sacramental* character. And with this we are indeed faced with the all-decisive question.

Only based on faith, of course, can it be declared that a certain observable action possesses sacramental quality or that there exists at all something that is a "sacrament", or what this might more specifically be. Yet even the nonbeliever may perhaps be expected at least to realize what the concept of "sacrament" means in the Christian—or rather Catholic—understanding. This concept declares that in a certain special and specific situation the "symbols" expressed through observable action and audible words not only *mean* something but also, by being acted out, transform this same meaning into objective *reality:* cleansing, forgiveness, nourishment through the Lord's true Body—*not,* however, flowing from the power of the human participants and much less from any potency inherent in those expressed symbols but coming exclusively from God's power, which is the one true effectiveness in any sacramental action. (Already I hear the battle cry "this is magic!" But discussing this particular topic will have to wait until later.)

Right here one other disputed aspect needs clarification. It has to be admitted that the very notion of a "sacrament" is preposterous indeed, and nobody can be pressured to accept it. But there should be absolute clarity concerning this point: if the sacred action, especially the Mass, were *not* a sacrament in this sense, that is, if in this action the unique and nonordinary divine presence were not truly achieved, then all our talk about the sacred would in fact be pointless, and all related manifestations, above all in the area of liturgy and cultus, would be so much pious folklore devoid of any relevant substance. Such folklore may at best appear worthy to be preserved for aesthetic or sentimental reasons but may much sooner fall victim, and rightly so, to the harsh realities of advancing history. All those "desacralization" crusades, especially when "theological" arguments are used, are ultimately rooted—as I am convinced—in just such a denial of any sacramental reality. They rest on the conviction that this action, perhaps still called "sacred", is in truth a purely human performance in which—objectively and independently from our imagination—*nothing at all happens,* least of all a real presence of the divine. The inescapable consequence of all this is rather obvious. Not only will it then become nonsense to perceive the edifice of a church as something other than a mere "human space", in the words of Harvey Cox. There will also, further and above all, no longer be any reason whatsoever to see the priest as someone "consecrated" and "set apart" for the sacred. And it would be difficult to shake my conviction that the ultimate and perhaps the only cause of that much-discussed "identity crisis" of the priesthood nowadays is anything else but the unwillingness or even inability—for several reasons—to acknowledge and accept the connection between the sacramental, consecrating action of the priest and the divine presence in the mystery of the Eucharistic sacrifice. Again, the inevitable consequence here is the need to find "new" definitions for the specific function of the priest and to find his proper mission in other areas: in the "ministry of the word", in "breaking the bread of Scripture", in "organizing the congregation", in social work, or even in the "revolution".

Those, in contrast, who hold fast to the conviction that in the sacred action, more specifically in the mystery of the Eucharist (foreshadowed, desired, and prefigured in all of mankind's cultic actions), there truly happens what is altogether exceptional, what is absolutely nonordinary: God's real presence among his people—those, of course, take it for granted that here the *separation* from the common routine of everyday life manifests and asserts itself more than clearly. *Rapi* (to be elevated and transported in rapture above the here and now)—this is for us men the very purpose of the divine presence, as the Church herself affirms.[22] Not that worldly things would be discredited by this; we are not led to disregard or to neglect them; instead, we are invited to value them correctly and transcend them. Incidentally, what the Greek Church Fathers have stated about religious feast days can be applied to sacred actions as well: they are not really "of this era or of this world".[23] In such actions there come about the true anticipation and inauguration of the future everlasting bliss at God's banquet table, an authentic *inchoatio vitae aeternae* (beginning of eternal life).

Whether the congregation sees itself as *parochia* (*paroikia*), an assembly of "strangers on earth", or as citizens of the promised Kingdom, in either

[22] Christmas Preface of the Roman Missal, which in essence proclaims the sacramental theme and thus is also used for Corpus Christi.

[23] See J. Pieper, *Zustimmung zur Welt. Eine Theorie des Festes,* 2nd ed. (Munich, 1964), 67f.

case it separates itself from the ordinary and everyday proceedings of secular society. And regardless
of the place where the liturgy is celebrated—in
a suburban makeshift chapel; on the dance floor
in a mission village; in a cathedral whose precious
adornments and stained glass windows symbolize
the heavenly Jerusalem; or in a concentration
camp, with a living wall of bodies creating for
a brief moment an intimate space barely shielded
from the intrusion of their torturers—one thing
is common to all these places: they are set apart,
no less by their simplicity than by their splendor
and magnificence, from the structure of everyday
existence, from its numbing misery as well as
from its deceptive complacency and ease.

And it is most natural for us to comport ourselves "differently" within such a separated precinct, not like in the sports arena, for instance,
or in the supermarket. There a "different" though
no less human language is used, "different" in
its manner, its inflection, its gestures, and its
vocabulary.

In opposition to this there are the proponents
of "desacralization", who, as is well known,
would rather see the Eucharist celebrated without
ceremonial language ("language" taken as all
forms of expression), just like any other common
meal in people's homes. The "presider" would

welcome the participants and express his joy at their presence, strangers would introduce themselves, and so on. The atmosphere of all this should be "festive" but in no wise "sacred". These proposals, indeed, are readily accepted. Thus a priest is considered especially progressive when he welcomes the faithful to Mass with the proper fashionable and commonplace greeting and when he dismisses them at the end not with the Church's required formula, "Go in peace", but rather, just like your friendly television announcer, wishing them from the altar "a pleasant evening". By all means and at any cost the sacred action must be incorporated into the ordinary daily activities, without "interfering" separation, and thus be made "truly human", as the expression goes.

The guiding principle here, besides being disgracefully wan and trite, rests on a deplorable misconception of the authentic nature of man, who in essence refuses to be "merely human" and who—so Pasqual—"infinitely transcends man". The sphere of a truly human existence extends far into further regions, and its life breath is definitely not sustained by the cozy atmosphere of the living room only. Thus my neighbor's private and personal affairs may arouse my interest much less than the truth that we both, he and I equally, are human beings "existing unto death",

created, fallen, redeemed, and now preparing together to receive the Bread of Life at God's table.
And if a celebration should be "festive" but not
"sacred", then I am tempted to turn this demand
around: "festivity" may be simply something
emotional, busy, subjective, while the "sacred"
action takes the solemnity of its stately form, transcending all individual peculiarities, and combines
it with that dispassionate serenity so typical of
all true dealings with reality.

Yet this is, once again, precisely the question
and the decisive point: Are we truly dealing here
with reality or only with mere "perceptions",
as Nietzsche puts it? The answer determines
everything else, including whether the boundary
lines between sacred and nonsacred domains are
acknowledged or not.

The early Church took such boundary lines
also as barriers that excluded those who did not
"belong" from participating in the sacred mysteries, even those who prepared for baptism, the
catechumens. For us latter-day Christians, used
as we are to taking the television broadcast of
the Mass for granted (too much so, perhaps),
this may be difficult to comprehend. All the same,
several things need to be considered here. First:
the first Christian communities never saw themselves as "exclusive clubs"; anybody was welcome

to join—not without proper initiation, though. Second: it is decisive what kind of reality is attributed to the celebration at hand. If it is no more than a common meal, although for "religious" purposes yet entirely at the disposal of the participants, then there exists no convincing reason why anybody should be excluded as long as he does not cause a disturbance. However, we may agree with the Church of the first centuries as well as the Second Vatican Council and hold that in the Eucharistic celebration God really becomes present and that those partaking of the sacred bread truly receive what the priest announces, the "Body of Christ". If so, then the entire situation changes profoundly. In this setting the Christian believer, as individual, can overcome the natural attitude of intense awe before God and dare to acknowledge and proclaim publicly, without embarrassment, the hidden foundation of his existence: "Lord, I am not worthy. . . ." This, however, inevitably leaves him extremely vulnerable and defenseless, in need of protection from outside uncommitted onlookers. At this point, we might at least realize that it would border on blasphemy to invite explicitly into the mystery someone who admittedly sees the proceedings at the altar as nothing but a more or less interesting instance of magic in action.

Magic?

But is not all that we mentioned here indeed simply magic? Is God made present in the celebration of certain rituals? Does eating the "sacred bread" effect real union with Christ, in whom the divine Logos has become man? Does not all this smack of magic? A meaningful discussion of this question is possible only if there exists some previous agreement, of course, as to the definition of "magic". One point is indeed right away clear to everybody: the concept is used as a denunciation; it is a term implying a reproach; "magic" is something that should not be found here.

An initial and quite useful definition goes like this: magic is the attempt to gain control, through certain rituals, over supernatural powers in order to make them serve human purposes. Magic, so understood, contrasts with the expression of true religion, which is worship, devotion, service. Magic is basically an attempt to dominate and take possession. Another aspect also transpires here: magic is not at all a mere subject matter for ethnology but rather a corruption of man's attitude toward God, and as such it is not confined to any specific time period. Moreover, by simply observing a specific ritual from the outside you will probably be unable to decide whether you witness "magic" or "religion".

Granted, someone may focus, say, on the concept of "sacrament" and ask the following question: Is it not the (Catholic) Church's own understanding of the sacred action that the specific divine presence in it is not brought about by the religious fervor of the priest, *ex opere operantis,* but rather *ex opere operato,* through the ritual action itself? And is this not, by definition, magic? This touches indeed an extremely important and very intricate aspect, which we are unable to discuss thoroughly here. We shall instead present four brief propositions intended to sum up in a nutshell the answer given by traditional sacramental theology.

First: The sacraments effect what they signify, not because of any human action, "religious" or otherwise, but because of God's gracious dispensation only. *Second*: "Effective *ex opere operato*" does not mean that the sacramental rite would not have to be also a true human act, implemented freely and deliberately and, furthermore, at least with the intention to do what the sacrament implies. *Third*: The one true agent in a sacrament, Christ himself, did indeed not intend to make his gifts for man contingent on the incidental disposition of his minister. *Fourth*: The effect of a sacrament is not "automatically" bestowed on the recipient but only when he willingly accepts it with devotion and faith.

All this, I have to admit, sounds altogether "unbelievable". I would not take it as true from anybody were it not based on the word of God. Magic, in any case, clearly does not enter here if the above-quoted definition is accepted, which does not necessarily mean that magical abuse and misconception would not be possible; on the contrary. It is precisely the aspect of *reality* in the sacramental rite, the only basis for everything truly sacred, that may foster also a *false* objectivization. Thus something purely material and observable—a ritual gesture, an architectural element, a specific time, for instance—may be attributed value in itself, isolating it from the living human action and from God's reality as well. Besides, no theology of the sacraments has ever taught God's gracious acts to be contingent on our liturgies, on sacred places and times, which nevertheless does not imply at all that we on our part would not be so conditioned either.

Yet we should discuss in further detail the topic of "magic". For there exists another, entirely different definition that applies this term to every "supernatural" reality extending into man's world and further to all events and facts "not resulting from the usual chain of cause and effect". This is the definition found in Johannes Hoffmeister's excellent philosophical dictionary.[24] And everything we are considering here, of course, would thus be relegated into the realm of "magic". Since this definition, too, preserves the negative overtones of the term *magic,* it clearly implies a denial of everything so labeled. This time, it is not emphasized that such a thing "should not be" but rather that a primitive mind may well take such a thing for "real", while in truth it is not. An example for this, in Rudolf Bultmann's words,[25] would be the belief that "a preexistent divine being appear on earth as a man" or that "a meal . . . confer spiritual strength". We may call all this "magical", or "mythical", or "archaic", no matter—it belongs on the long list of discarded conceptions. All this, as is affirmed here, has ultimately no reality at all. Not even prayer is conceived as piercing "vertically" through the confines of our closed human world. Only the

[24] J. Hoffmeister, *Wörterbuch der philosophischen Begriffe* (Hamburg, 1955), 390.
[25] R. Bultmann, "Neues Testament und Mythologie", in *Kerygma und Mythos,* ed. H. W. Bartsch (Hamburg and Bergstedt, 1967), 15, 19.

discussion, in ethical or political terms, of what passes as contemporary topics may claim to be "prayer without magic". Whoever is willing to subscribe to such a definition of "magic", this is obvious, has just about denied, or at best ignored, the specific aspect of reality that is the foundation not only of any concept of the sacred but also of the Christian world view as such.

Regardless whether "desacralization" is meant as a factual occurrence or a program, it usually includes "heresies", not only theological but also philosophical and specifically anthropological heresies.

Someone who does not acknowledge that the nature of man does not contain anything "purely spiritual" or anything "purely corporeal" is of course unable to appreciate or enter into "that structure of visible and sense-related forms" we call a "sacred rite".[26] *Anima forma corporis* (the soul is the life form of the body) is an old expression, frequently forgotten or even rejected by Christianity yet confirmed daily by empirical findings about man's true nature. And this prin-

---

[26] J. A. Jungmann, "Sinn und Probleme des Kultes", in *Der Kult und der heutige Mensch,* ed. M. Schmaus and K. Forster (Munich, 1961), 5.

ciple, as Romano Guardini aptly points out, provides the foundation for all liturgical considerations.[27] It is indeed a key principle: as one "grasps" it or not, so will the passage into the realm of the sacred be opened or closed.

Only in view of this principle, for example, will the strict formality of all sacred "language" (gestures, signs, words) find its explanation. This definite form is not only necessitated by the communal character of the sacred action, although it is true that free improvisation, on the spur of the moment, would always be the action of the individual only. No, such formality has perhaps more to do with an inherent quality of not being at any one's disposal, the same way a completed poem may not be changed at will.

Obviously, the twofold truth of the principle, *anima forma corporis,* can be denied in an equally twofold way: either by extreme "spiritualism" or, at the other end of the spectrum, by what may be called "corporealism". The former considers the mental attitude as the only aspect that matters and therefore holds the manner how it is expressed to be merely "external" and thus inconsequential. The latter also insists, for entirely

[27] R. Guardini, *Liturgie und liturgische Bildung,* 38ff.

different reasons though, on the absolutely contingent character of all verbal and tangible expressions. Structural rituals are seen as intolerable
impositions; even congregational singing becomes "manipulation". Praised instead as being
"authentic" is the attitude of following the "pull
of the moment" and accepting no restraints. Dis-
turbingly, both forms of denial lead in practice
to almost identical consequences. Neither "spiritualism" nor "corporealism" recognizes the
unique opportunity for the individual to transcend the confines of his own subjective self precisely by accepting the communal challenge and
entering into the objective form of a structured
and stately ritual.

Above all, those who deny the principle of
anima forma corporis will never understand one of
the fundamental concepts in the realm of the sacred: the reality of the *symbol*. They will never
realize how entirely normal it is for man to act
not merely with a practical goal in mind but also,
every now and then, with the intention of setting
a sign—be this only the gesture of lighting a can-
dle, *not* to brighten the room but rather to express
the festive atmosphere of the moment, or of re-
membering a deceased loved one or of offering
worship and thanksgiving.

Man's Poverty and Richness

The explicit "uselessness" of all this reminds us of one other aspect found in the symbolic action: the aspect of abundance and enthusiasm, of generosity and almost extravagance. The first draught of wine from the jug is not "used", not consumed, but "wasted" and poured out on the waves or the floor as an offering to the gods. People erect not merely a functional meeting hall but the basilica of Ronchamp or a cathedral. And, of course, the pealing bells of Notre Dame were never, at least not primarily, intended simply to proclaim the time of day or some special event (otherwise, the era of the wristwatch would indeed have rendered them superfluous); no, they have always been and still are the expression of non-verbal jubilation, representing exuberance and largesse.

But is not the counterargument that advocates simplicity, even poverty, also justified? I do not hesitate to answer with an emphatic yes; this argument indeed has a point. I do not believe, however, that the constructive tension embracing frugality as well as pomp and circumstance can ever find an undisputed, harmonious resolution; it will always stay with us. Josef Andreas Jungmann,[28] too, lists this tension among seven or eight inner conflicts that are inherent in the nature of all cultic action. Rejoicing that is skimping and sparing is no rejoicing at all. Yet again, splendor and magnificence do not necessarily mean extravagant expenses, though such are not excluded. In no wise, of course, should that kind of extravagance considered here be construed as an ostentatious display of wealth and riches. We mean the spontaneous expression of an inner richness, indeed, of *that* richness flowing from experiencing the true presence of God among his people. This identifies once again the only and enduring core of all that is "sacred", without which it would never be more than habit or fancy, mere "performance" and "show", perhaps still impressive but in essence without any real foundation.

At the same time there appear here images of extreme human privation, of misery, not of the material but rather of the existential kind. Imagine a world full of useful and disposable things but devoid of anything that could kindle utterly disinterested rejoicing; replete with science but without philosophical reflection on the meaning of it all; with plenty of research but without historical awareness; with entertainment and daily fun but

[28] J. A. Jungmann, "Sinn und Probleme des Kultes", 9f.

without a true feast day, without great poetry and music. If such a world appears depressing, then this other situation would be reason for outright despair: to be imprisoned by a desacralized and entirely "secular" world, without the possibility of transcending the immediate demands of daily life by acknowledging the much greater and fuller dimensions of our existence and claiming them as our true human endowment. Such "stepping beyond", then, would happen not only in philosophical reflection, not only in poetic emotion, but also *realiter* (in living terms), in the setting of life itself, and especially in the sacred action.

Postscript

Against these considerations on the sacred and desacralization, a theologian critic, in a magazine for priests, has raised two objections: first, the contemporary discussion is ignored; and second, the "biblical argumentation" is missing. I responded as follows.

1. It is debatable what *the* contemporary discussion might be. Still, the experience of deep dissensions did in fact prompt my remarks. *On the one hand,* I witness the demands for "desacralization", advanced for some years now by a group of Cath-

olic theologians. Though divergent in specifics, these demands agree in their basic thrust: against the traditional structure and form of liturgical rites; against the "sacred" language of the *verba certa et solemnia,* the prescribed and solemn formulas; against the ceremonial form of symbolic gestures and actions; against houses of worship that in structure and function are purposely distinct from residential, industrial, or office buildings; and not least against the image of the priest as a "consecrated" person, specifically ordained for the celebration of the sacramental mysteries. *On the other hand,* I am aware of the explicit determination with which the Church herself, despite flexibility in details, insists on all these things, unswervingly up to the latest pronouncements (so, for instance, in the decrees of the Second Vatican Council or in the *Institutio Generalis* of April 1969 concerning the revised order of the Mass). There we read that the outward liturgical signs both express and accomplish man's sanctification and that the liturgy itself is a "sacred action surpassing all others",[29] "the summit" of the Church's activity and the "fount from which all her powers flow".[30] There we find binding

---

[29] "Actio sacra praecellenter", *Constitution on the Sacred Liturgy* (hereafter *CSL*), art. 7.

[30] *CSL*, art. 10.

norms, for instance, regarding the celebration of
the Eucharist, determining not only the words
to be used but also its external form (including
singing, kneeling, posture of the priest, kissing
the altar, sign of the Cross, and so forth).[31] There
the church building is seen not at all as a "functional hall" but, on the contrary, is called *aedes
sacra* (sacred edifice), and its "solemn dedication"
is taken for granted, as is that of the altar.[32] There
we hear about the "dignity of the place of worship,"[33] about "sacred" vessels and vestments.[34]
And, of course, there the priests are called neither
presbyters nor indeed parochial presiders but *sacerdotes* and *ministri sacri*.

This, then, is the "controversy" on which I,
as an observer deeply involved and perturbed,
have voiced my opinion. I should immediately
add, however, that I do not see a true "controversy" here or a real "discussion", of course.
There simply cannot be a "discussion" in the strict
sense between the Church, when speaking in profound self-expression, and a theological school
of thought, no matter how much the latter may
dominate the news. And in speaking out I did

[31] *CSL,* art. 22; *Institutio Generalis* (hereafter *IG*), nos. 19ff.
[32] *IG,* nos. 255, 262, 265.
[33] *IG,* no. 279.
[34] *IG,* nos. 289, 297.

not at all intend to interfere in such a "discussion", as if weighing the arguments of one side against the other.

2. My considerations centered primarily on philosophical and anthropological aspects. I intended to clarify two points: *First,* the "desacralization" proponents, with their tendency to dismantle all boundaries between "sacred" and "profane", find themselves in peculiar company, a situation that unexpectedly sheds a different light on the issue they raise. They find themselves of one mind with a direction in poetics that denies the difference between poetry and prose, thus denying poetry itself. They further are in line with a certain philosophy of science that aims to reduce philosophy to "exact science", thus destroying philosophy itself. These theories have one thing in common: they all proclaim a "one-dimensional" closed realm of human existence (making it a mere difference in words whether they declare prose to be poetry, science to be philosophy, the profane to be sacred, or vice versa). *Second,* I wanted to bring out how utterly inhumane such leveling tendencies really are. Above all, I intended to show how much the Church's teaching and practice conform to the true nature of man. And this Church, throughout her history, has never wavered in proclaiming the sacred to be

in its own right and in acting accordingly. In other words, I wanted to point to the absolute and fundamental principle, also in this context, that grace never destroys but rather presupposes what is rooted in "nature", that is, in the order of creation. You do not have to be a Christian to know the concept of "sign", but without this knowledge you will never understand the concept of "sacrament". I thus found it unavoidable to mention *pre*theological and *pre*-Christian categories (*témenos* [symbol] and *anima forma corporis* [presence of the divine]).

3. This clarification may also explain the criticized absence of "biblical argumentation". In a primarily philosophical essay such argumentation would appear not only superfluous but also out of place.

Still, I do not have the slightest doubt that the Church's liturgy and the doctrine incorporated in it do not merely rest on "biblical argumentation" but that they in themselves *constitute* no less than the authentic interpretation of Christ's revelation, safeguarded by the Author himself. A situation where priests and theologians argue against this by quoting the New Testament offers, in my opinion, a depressing spectacle. True, often enough the shaky character of such arguments is rather obvious. For example, the New Testa-

ment indeed reports that Jesus Christ calls us his
brothers. Yet it also says that he calls himself a
king; that he approves when the disciples address
him as Master and Lord; that the apostles, whenever his true nature shines through, fall down
in worship; that angels come and serve him. And
further, to justify the "emancipation of the sacred", the torn temple curtain is invariably quoted
and interpreted accordingly. Yet Tradition would
easily provide half a dozen entirely different and
equally "convincing" interpretations. Or then,
the image of God's temple, as a temple "we are
ourselves", known already in Jewish tradition,
clearly does not imply a rejection of ritual devotion. And so forth.

All the same, confronted with a confusing array
of exegetical claims, the layman and perhaps also
the theologian, in order to save his faith, can do
little else (it suffices, though) but rely on that
particular interpretation of Scripture manifested
"in the self-expression of the Church", to use
Cardinal Hermann Volk's words. Profound wari-
ness is in order concerning any "biblical argumentation" that is at odds with such living exegesis.

CHAPTER TWO

WHAT MAKES A PRIEST?

IN WHAT CONSISTS the distinctive difference between priest and nonpriest? Imagine someone, when asked about the specific characteristics of a licensed physician, who responds with the reminder that the art of healing would not be limited to the medical profession alone, that there are many "gifted" and knowledgeable nonprofessionals, that every good mother would know how to dress a wound, and so on. Then someone else might declare that a physician, in actual fact, would always be, at the same time and in addition, a citizen, a husband or wife, a father, a neighbor, frequently also the director of a hospital and thus some kind of manager, and so on. Now, both answers would indeed contain something entirely correct, and yet both answers would clearly have missed the point of the question. They would not have given an answer at all.

Something very similar happens quite often, I think, in the discussions concerning the priesthood. Our example using the "physician" could adequately be answered more or less in this way: the specific distinction of the licensed physician consists in a legally recognized education, which

First published in *Hochland* 63 (1971) with the title "Was unterscheidet den Priester?" Later published by Verlag der Arche (Zurich, 1971) under the same title.

authorizes him, say, to cut someone open (anyone else would be prosecuted for infliction of injury); to prescribe medications, even those containing poison; to declare a person legally dead; and so forth. In just the same way the question as to what makes a priest aims not at all at uncovering the factual variety of priestly ministries, or the specific challenges of the "modern priest", or the priestly call of every Christian. If this truth were considered and acknowledged more rigorously, then various inconsistencies in the contemporary discussion would disappear almost instantly.

We witness perplexing and vehement attacks on what is contemptuously called "conceptual constriction", meaning the attempt to focus the discussion on the specific ministry reserved for the priest, and the priest *alone,* in contrast to the laity. Yet such "constriction" is in truth as indispensable as it is clarifying—with the understanding, of course, that a description of the *differentia specifica* (specific distinction) alone and in itself does neither pretend nor desire to paint a complete "image" of the priest.

Commissioned and Consecrated

The question, incidentally, as to what distinguishes the priest from a layman can be reformu-

lated without change of its meaning, namely, thus:
What, actually, is happening in the priestly ordination? The occasional observation or even com-
plaint regarding the absence in contemporary
theological thought of any worthwhile reflection
on the subject of priestly ordination may well
be justified. Indeed, the otherwise abundantly
sprouting literature on the priesthood says precious little about this sacrament, alarmingly little,
I should say. Nonetheless, it would of course
be absurd to conclude that the Church's teaching
and traditional theology would not contain a suffi-
ciently detailed conception of what happens when
the bishop ordains a priest and what the priest
receives in this liturgical rite.

The literal meaning of the terms *ordo* and *ordina-
tio* does not, however, yield much information
at first. It rather suggests a mere act of administra-
tion and organization, assigning someone a particular function. And something of that sort is indeed
happening there: the priest, through ordination,
is being "commissioned", put in charge, dele-
gated, and called to fill a certain office; he is ap-
pointed, assigned, and sent forth. Still, the
preferred term to describe what happens in the
sacrament of *ordination,* used already in early theological texts and then emphatically and frequently
by the Second Vatican Council, conveys and un-

derlines a further, quite different meaning. This term is *consecration*. *Sacerdotes consecrantur,*[1] priests are *consecrated*. And with this, as we have indicated, there opens up a further dimension missing in all the other terms listed above. It is precisely this new and fundamentally different element in the concept of ordination and priesthood as such that causes the contemporary controversy.

Term and concept of *consecratio,* of course, are no new invention; they are, on the contrary, very old. *Consecratio* was first and foremost an "essential term" in the cultic language of ancient Rome; it soon found its way into the language of Christianity, after the danger of false connotations and "misconceptions no longer existed", readily to become a "common liturgical term".[2] Inciden-

---

[1] Thomas Aquinas, *Summa theologica* 3, 67, 2; *Summa contra Gentes* 4, 77. "Presbyteri consecrantur ut veri sacerdotes Novi Testamenti". *Dogmatic Constitution on the Church,* art. 28. Similar formulations are found in the *Decree on the Ministry and Life of Priests,* arts. 5 and 12. It is difficult to understand what Ivan D. Illich is trying to say with his evidently polemical notions of "laymen consecrated for an office" or even "the sacramental office of laymen". After all, the priest, through the sacrament of ordination, is indeed nothing else but a "layman consecrated for an office"! See Ivan D. Illich, "Das Verschwinden des Priesters", in *Almosen und Folter* (Munich, 1970), 68f.

[2] *Reallexikon für Antike und Christentum,* ed. Theodor Klauser (Stuttgart: A. Hiersemann, n.d.), 3:269, 276ff.

tally, the New Testament derives its titles for ecclesiastical offices not from the Jewish or Gentile cultic terminology of the time but from the secular realm of the political order. This proven fact, however, in my opinion, does not carry such an obvious significance as is frequently supposed. The intention evidently was to prevent all possibility of confusing the new Christian dispensation with the Mosaic rites of the temple or, even more importantly, with pagan cultic terms. Does not every "first generation" find itself in such a unique situation, its identity precarious and threatened? I know of a European Catholic missionary, working for decades in India, who had the sacred *om* of Hinduism (in Bengal script rendered with *three* letters) engraved on the base of his chalice as a symbol of the Trinity. Yet for a newly converted Hindu this would be inappropriate. His first and decisive concern has to concentrate on living out and clarifying the radically new demands of his young Christian faith, and so he must first turn away entirely from his "former" ways and avoid confusion between the "new" and the "old".

The missionary, in contrast, can afford to be open-minded in this respect since his faith is not imperiled here; he is right in emphasizing common ground in spite of all differences. And since in the celebration of the Christian mysteries the rites of the temple and all pagan cults were not only supplanted but at the same time also purified, corrected, perfected, and fulfilled, it became possible for later generations in the early Church, rightfully and in all sincerity, to adopt into their own language quite a number of expressions from Jewish as well as pagan rituals, without having to fear confusing misconceptions anymore.

We should point out here, in passing, as it were, that we no longer have any direct knowledge about the "connotations", the contexts and implications, of those designations taken from the political sphere, or of how they were used in the living language of the first century. Those, however, who nowadays speak of the bishop as the "supervisor", or of the priest as the "presider at the Eucharistic assembly", are simply using a stylish "jargon" aimed not so much at defining a situation as at hitting an opposing position.

Not unlike concepts such as "sign", "symbol", "sacrifice", so also is *consecratio* apparently rooted in a "natural" and insofar *pre*-Christian way of thinking. Concepts of this kind, like everything on a "natural" level, have to be corrected in light of the Faith and may perhaps require cleansing from their demonic corruption and distortion in order to restore their authentic meaning. Such concepts, however, are a necessary foundation, a precondition, without which the new dimension of reality, opened up by Christ, would also remain inaccessible.

What, then, is the concrete meaning of *consecratio?* Neither the Jew of the Old Testament nor the devout Greek or Roman would have needed such an explanation. But the Christian of our own days, especially if he is interested in theology, must first overcome his "suspicion of mythology" before being able to shed a certain bias and accept—or at least more or less understand—what the Church herself, in teaching and sacramental practice, has confidently declared her patrimony throughout the centuries. We are compelled, once again, to employ a short and elementary primer, as it were, in order to regain what our generation has just about lost. To be precise, we are dealing here with a two-sided reality. *Consecratio* constitutes only one side of the coin,[3] *dedicatio* the other. Both concepts are intimately related in the German language: either one is correctly rendered by *Weihung.*

Dedicatio is by its nature the primary and preceding of the two concepts. It applies when man "dedicates" and "presents" a "votive offering" to God, be it a part of his possessions or else

[3] See *Oxford Classical Dictionary* (1957), 259.

his very self. *Dedicatio* declares that this offering,
this sanctified gift, has been explicitly and defini-
tively removed from common usage and from
the usual utilitarian purpose. A church building
erected with donations from the congregation,
for example, may in this sense be considered a
votive offering, that is, something "dedicated"
even *before* any solemn dedication by the bishop
and apart from it. An object thus removed from
all utilitarian purposes has not yet, by this alone,
become a *res sacra* (sacred object);[4] such transformation occurs specifically in the *consecratio*, which
in its nature is not a private or even a human
rite, since its justification derives from higher authority. In Rome, as the ancient jurist Gaius men-
tions in his *Institutions*,[5] a thing would be
considered *sacrum* only after it had been "consecrated by authority of the Roman people"—
the latter representing not a mere political but
also in true fact a cultural and religious community.

And so we find these two aspects also in the
priestly ordination. The first is the *dedicatio*, the

---

[4] *Reallexikon für Antike und Christentum*, 3:643f. *Oxford Classical Dictionary*, s.v. "consecratio".

[5] *Institutionum commentarii quattuor* 2, 5.

dedication, the self-sacrifice, by which the candidate in an act of extreme "nonconformism" renounces explicitly and permanently the common standards of a life aimed at "making a living" and "being useful to society" and at the same time vows himself to the exclusive service of God. The Second Vatican Council spells it out: their very ministry makes a special claim on priests "not to conform themselves to this world".[6] The second aspect is the *consecratio* proper, the consecration of the one who offers himself. The Council, again, states that this consecration is accomplished "by God through the ministry of the bishop",[7] God, as it were, accepting the candidate's "dedication" and ratifying it in the fullness of his final "consecration".

It is precisely here that the decisive difference between commissioning and consecration becomes evident: the one accepting a commission is not changed in his inner nature, while the one being consecrated receives a new and essential

[6] See Rom 12:2. *Decree on the Ministry and Life of Priests,* art. 3.

[7] "Presbyteri a Deo, ministrante Episcopo, consecrantur". *Presbyterorum ordinis, The Decree on the Ministry and Life of Priests,* art. 5.

inner quality—the consecration transforms him into a *persona sacra*.

We find it exceedingly difficult, no matter in what context, to translate the expression *persona sacra* in an adequate way. "Sacred person" would be an awkward rendering, though literally correct; to use "holy" or "sanctified person" appears even less acceptable. The official German version of *Presbyterorum ordinis, The Decree on the Ministry and Life of Priests,* calls the *ministri sacri* "Diener am Heiligen"[8] (ministers of the sacred), which makes sense yet still remains an incorrect translation. The most acceptable solution may be to call the priest a "consecrated person" (German: "einen Geweihten"; the English translation has "sacred minister").

Here, two considerations should be kept clearly in mind. *First* of all, "consecration" indicates an objective, inherent quality. It obligates its bearer to a life worthy of a "minister of the sacred", yet it is not contingent on such subjective worthiness. Just so would the respect owed the priest by the faithful be aimed, of course, at the specific quality conferred in the *consecratio* (which still re-

---

[8] *Decree on the Ministry and Life of Priests,* art. 19.

mains outside the free disposal of the recipient)[9] and not at any moral perfection or intellectual excellence. It is, incidentally, none other than Goethe who in his *Dichtung und Wahrheit* (Poetry and truth),[10] in a clearly polemical section on the Catholic doctrine of the seven sacraments, sings the praises of precisely this aspect of priestly ordination, the objective and noncontingent nature of "consecration".

And *second,* we have to be aware that such *consecratio* can be conferred only once; it is by nature irrevocable and final: "Once consecrated, always consecrated."[11] I would step outside the field of my competence were I to try a specific discussion of the "indelible seal", the *character indelebilis,* conferred in priestly ordination. But I am quite certain that nobody could say anything of substance in this regard without having first explored the concept and reality of *consecratio.*

Still, being a "consecrated person" is not, as

[9] It is not a *virtus* that has become an essential part of the priest's inner self but rather a *virtus instrumentalis,* according to Thomas Aquinas. See *Summa theologica* 3, 63, 5 ad 1.

[10] J. W. Goethe, *Dichtung und Wahrheit,* pt. II, bk. 7.

[11] "Nihil consecratum iterato consecratur". Thomas Aquinas, *Summa contra Gentes* 4, 77.

such, the essential distinction of the priest, not-withstanding the fact that the mark conferred on him through the bishop's consecration affects and determines his identity more than any mere outward commissioning could. This is not yet the *differentia specifica,* the specific and formal distinction we are looking for. The essential distinction of the priest rather consists in a special spiritual authority invested in him through his ordination, a *potestas sacra*[12] (sacred power), in the Council's words. Thomas Aquinas offers one of his succinct descriptions in this regard: the authority bestowed on the priest in ordination, he says, is his power to celebrate the Eucharist, *in persona Christi* and for the universal Church.[13] There is *no question* that the exercise of this authority means "service"; it "serves" to make God's incarnate Logos, in sacramental signs, present among men. Such service happens in the very fact of a priest's celebrating and dispensing the Eucharistic mysteries or any of the other sacraments. The question of "authority and service" in a social and sociological context lies on an entirely different level and has

[12] *Dogmatic Constitution on the Church,* art. 10.

[13] "Sacerdoti, cum ordinatur, confertur potestas hoc sacramentum [= Eucharistiae] consecrandi in persona Christi". *Summa theologica* 3, 82, 1.

no bearing at all on the much more fundamental reality discussed here. This sociological level, of course, has its own importance. On this level, attitudes such as collegiality, compassion, and nonconformity with the privileged are indispensable, and yet such requirements do not really touch on the status and authority of the *potestas sacra*. But then, I do not think you would have found in the past many "lordly reverends" who refused to get up in the middle of the night to bring the Viaticum to even the poorest members of their "flock".

Thomas Aquinas' fundamental statement explicitly claims to identify the core of the question. His answer combines two thoughts, and we shall briefly consider each: first, the priest as acting "in place of Christ", and then the intimate relationship between priesthood and the Eucharist.

"In Persona Christi"

Someone speaks or acts "in the person of" someone else: different languages everywhere use this expressive image, thus showing it to be, once again, a pre-Christian and pretheological expression. It seems, like the term *persona* (mask), to stem originally from the world of the theater, but it is also regularly used in legal contexts. In both instances it means a particular manner of identification, of representation. Classic Roman literature, as the respective dictionaries show, used this expression in many different constructions. But even the late Latin of the Vulgate version of the New Testament contains, just this one time, such a construction. Paul, in Second Corinthians (2:10), writes: "I have forgiven you *in persona Christi.*" The Latin theology of patristic and medieval times, naturally enough, understood Paul here as saying, "not on my own but on Christ's authority".[14] And Luther's Bible, like most German translations up to the nineteenth century, has *an Christi statt* (in place of Christ). A more accurate rendering of this passage, however, based on the Greek original (*en prosōpo Christoū,* before the face of Christ),[15] would be "in the presence of Christ."

The question remains, though, whether our

---

[14] See Thomas Aquinas, *Commentary on 2 Corinthians,* chap. 2, lect. 2; also *Summa theologica* 3, 22, 4; and Augustine, *Serm.* 210, 6, 9 (Migne), PL 38, 1052.

[15] The almost identical meaning of the terms *persona* and *prōsopon* notwithstanding, the Greek language does not possess an expression that would be analogous to the meaning of *in persona alicujus agere.* See Siegmund Schlossmann, *Persona und Prōsopon im Recht und im christlichen Dogma* (Kiel, 1906), 39.

rendering "in place of someone" accurately captures and expresses the meaning of *in persona alicujus*. For instance, when I say in the course of a conversation, "To be or not to be—that is the question", I quote Shakespeare. But the actor on the stage, pronouncing the same words, does not "quote" Shakespeare or any of his creations; he rather speaks and acts "in the person" of Hamlet, whom he "personifies". Even more accurately, he does not speak and act "in place of Hamlet" but rather identifies with him in a certain sense; he speaks and acts "as Hamlet".

Christian theology has accepted this particular expression in all innocence in order to emphasize through it the special relationship between the ordained priest and the person of Christ.

The words of Christ "this is my Body" could very well be used merely as a quotation—perhaps during an exercise at a seminar on the history of religion, in connection with a discussion of the Last Supper account in Matthew's Gospel. Something quite different would happen, intrinsically different, if these same words were to be read explicitly as "Sacred Scripture" in a group of believing Christians gathered for Bible study. And these words would once again mean something new and different when "proclaimed" within the liturgy of the word, either by a commissioned lector or by the priest himself. And yet, we would still deal here with some kind of "quotation", meaning: thus spoke Jesus the night before he died. All the same, in the sequence of these three examples the existential closeness to the one and authentic Author of those words, Christ himself, grows progressively more intimate and, as it were, more intensive. Still, only when the priest, celebrating the Eucharistic mystery, pronounces these very same words as part of the Eucharistic Prayer, only then does he specifically and authentically speak and act *in persona Christi,* in the person of Christ. Something of an entirely different quality is happening here, something of a new reality that simply does not fit any longer into the category of "quotation". For here the basis for what is spoken and done is a true identification, far above and beyond the case of an actor impersonating a stage character, which would be closer to our understanding. No, it is not the priest who would bring about this identity, perhaps by "slipping into the role" of Christ in his thoughts and feelings. It is rather Christ himself who effects this identity, he who "in the sacrifice of the Mass . . . is present in the person of the priest",[16] to quote Vatican II.

[16] "Praesens adest . . . in ministri persona". *Constitution on the Sacred Liturgy,* art. 7.

No lengthy explanation is needed to point out how far all these things are removed, perhaps more than ever before in history, from the common way of thinking found in contemporary man—but, of course, only if they are taken as indeed they demand, for solid and salvific reality, not for mere images, metaphors, or allegories. This specific identification we are discussing here not only defies definition in psychological terms; it lies altogether beyond the realm of empirical verification. The reality involved is accessible, no matter how imperfectly, by faith alone; yet it is, nevertheless, in a strict sense "true" reality. Someone may be utterly unable to understand and to accept, at least as a meaningful possibility, what happens in the celebration of the Eucharistic mystery, namely, the identification of Christ with the priest who speaks and acts "in his person". Such a one seems equally unable so much as to conceive of those specific realities expressed and at the same time concealed in notions such as Incarnation, Church, and sacrament.

Tied to the Eucharist

The Second Vatican Council declared the liturgy of the Eucharist to be *culmen et fons,* the "summit toward which the activity of the Church is directed", and also "the fount from which all her powers flow".[17] Understanding the reality of the Eucharist, above all, remains by necessity beyond the ability of those who categorically reject even the possibility of that mystical yet real identification of Christ with the ordained priest. Thomas Aquinas gives two reasons for this, which all too often seem to be overlooked. We should recall here that the sacraments as such, and also the Church, are for Thomas the means by which the Incarnation of the divine Logos is sustained and perpetuated throughout history.

First, he declares the Eucharist to be the most prominent of all the sacraments, comparable to bread, the most prominent of all foods.[18] In the Eucharist, all the other sacraments are comprised and perfected.[19] It possesses "a dignity so high that it cannot be enacted except in the person of Christ himself" (*nisi in persona Christi*).[20] Second, it follows from this that in all the other sacraments, except in the Eucharist, the priest speaks as him-

---

[17] *Constitution on the Sacred Liturgy*, art. 10.

[18] *Summa theologica* 2, 2, 83, 9.

[19] *Summa contra Gentes* 4, 74. Similar in Thomas Aquinas, *Scripta super libros Sententiarum* 4 d. 24, 2, 1.

[20] *Summa theologica* 3, 82, 1.

self. Whether he says, "I baptize you . . . ," or, "I absolve you . . . ", in each of these instances the words *ex persona ministri,* namely, coming solely from the speaker, a human being, are pronounced. In the Eucharist alone are the form-giving words pronounced in such a manner as if Christ himself were the speaker—"which is made clear to us by the fact that the priest in the actualization of this sacrament does nothing else but pronounce Christ's own words".[21]

We should be aware of the various differentiated and graduated ways a priest can be related to his own words. He may pray at Mass, "Let your Spirit come upon these gifts to make them holy, so that they may become for us the Body and Blood of our Lord, Jesus Christ." This is obviously, in its entire thrust, a prayer totally different from the one he recites before receiving Communion, when he asks that the reception of Christ's

---

[21] *Summa theologica* 3, 78, 1. If this is truly understood, then the German rendering of *"in persona Christi"* as *"in der Rolle Christi",* as found in the official translation of Vatican II's *Constitution on the Sacred Liturgy* (art. 33), will appear at least questionable, if not outright false. A rendering totally faithful to the original is perhaps possible only in some paraphrasing, such as "in the name and the power of Christ". (The English translation of this passage reads "in the person of Christ".)

Body and Blood "may not bring me condemna-
tion but health in mind and body". The latter,
in contrast to the former, is a genuine prayer of
petition that expresses his personal trust and hope.
The actual and individual personality of the priest
is equally not in the least blotted out but, on
the contrary, challenged to fullest involvement
whenever he holds the bread and, *in persona
Christi,* pronounces the words, "This is my
Body."

This challenge, addressed to our contemporary
critical mentality, to the Christian as such, and
especially to the priest, may well on occasion grow
to the limit (and even beyond the limit) of human
endurance—something quite understandable. Decisive here is, as in so many things, whether a
person is capable of mustering a genuine faith,
which basically means accepting as established
and objective reality—that is, mind independent
and existing in itself—all this: God himself; the
Incarnation and its continuation in the living
Church; the seven sacraments, especially Christ's
real presence in the Eucharist and also, though
differently, in the ordained priest's celebrating the
Eucharist. Only if this prerequisite is fulfilled can
it at all be expected that such certitude breaks
forth from the inner recesses of the believer to
determine and mold, as is entirely natural in every

other respect as well, a person's outward behavior and comportment—including the manner of speech and gestures, even the seemingly inconsequential area of dress and vestment.[22] The liturgical vestments, indeed, took their specific form, not because of any practical need stemming from their specific use, but rather because of their historical and cultural environment. And yet, they proclaim loud and clear that, for a certain span of time, their wearer is speaking and acting *not* as the individual named and described on his driver's license but *in persona Christi*. For this reason is it a much more serious matter than simply bad judgment or poor style when the priest at the altar greets the congregation like a "good buddy", using some conventional commonplace—something a serious actor, for instance, would never do onstage. The same has to be said regarding the priest who after the liturgy, still dressed in his vestments, joins the chatting groups of people outside the church to discuss the weather and the latest news. An American friend from New Mexico and I had some common experiences in this regard. He was fluent in Spanish and after years of study an expert on this subject. He told

[22] See Erik Peterson, "Theologie des Kleides", in *Marginalien zur Theologie* (Munich, 1956).

me—and this contrasts with the preceding remarks—that the Indians, many of whom were
his personal friends, would ignore him as soon
as they had donned their ceremonial robes and
would not engage in their usual friendly conversation with him.

The one fact, now, that the priest in celebrating
the Eucharistic mystery "acts in Christ's stead",[23]
in persona Christi: this fact has to be seen as the
specific quality setting the ordained priest apart
from the laity. The latter, of course, because of
baptism, can also claim a "priestly" name and
quality; neither medieval theology nor the
Counter-reformation ever ignored the doctrine of
the common priesthood of all believers. Thomas
Aquinas, for example, quotes with approval the
statement attributed to Chrysostom that "every
saint is a priest" and adds that a layman united
with Christ in faith and love would indeed possess
a "spiritual priesthood".[24] And the *Catechismus
Romanus,* inspired by the Council of Trent, contains this affirmation: "All the believers . . . are
called 'priests'."[25] What the consecrated priest receives in the sacrament of ordination, however,

---

[23] Cyprian, *Epist.* 63, 14 (Migne), PL 4, 397.
[24] *Summa theologica* 3, 82, 1 ad 2.
[25] 2:7, 23.

namely, the authority to celebrate for the entire Church the Eucharist *in persona Christi,* precisely this authority can "in no wise" be claimed by the laity, as the Church has insistently declared.

Priestly Action and Actions of Priests

At this point we have to make a distinction between genuine priestly action and the activities of priests. Analogous to the ancient distinction setting "human actions" proper, the *actus humanus,* apart from "actions of humans", we could equally distinguish between specifically priestly actions and those actions that simply happen to be performed by a priest. These latter actions do not flow from the authority of the priestly office, nor should they be evaluated by any other but their own inherent criteria. Traditionally the first element of this distinction is subdivided, for good reasons, into priestly actions in a strict sense, actions that are, therefore, *primarily* priestly, and an area of subordinated and *secondary* yet no less priestly actions. Thus we would consider, in effect, *three* different areas in which priestly actions unfold. I deem it worthwhile to consider more closely this distinction, which may at first appear rather pedantic; it should shed some light on the question that is our topic here.

The *primary* area of priestly action is described in the following two statements; though separated by seven hundred years, they both express exactly the same thought: "A priest is ordained to celebrate the sacrament of Christ's Body and Blood."[26] And the second statement: "It is in the Eucharistic cult . . . that they [the priests] exercise in a supreme degree [*maxime*] their sacred functions."[27] (It should be noted here that the author of the first statement, Thomas Aquinas, in clear accord with Vatican II understands the Eucharist not at all as limited to the consecration and only affecting the "material" species of bread and wine. He explicitly sees the "Sacrament of Christ's Body" also as the sacrament of love[28] and peace,[29] and above all as the sacrament of Church unity, by whose power "the many are united in Christ".)[30] To celebrate this *mysterium,* both statements assert, would be the *primary* function of priestly existence.

There is no doubt, to be sure, that the decrees of Vatican II explicitly emphasize also the *ministry of the word.* The respective context, however, clari-

---

[26] *Summa theologica* 3, 67, 2.

[27] *Dogmatic Constitution on the Church,* art. 28

[28] *Summa theologica* 3, 73, 3 ad 3.

[29] *Scripta super libros Sententiarum* 4 d. 25, 2, 2, 2.

[30] *Summa theologica* 3, 82, 2 ad 3; 67, 2; 73, 4.

fies this to mean a *priority of sequence*. Since faith comes from hearing, salvation *begins* with the proclamation of the word, and so proclamation, indeed, comes first. We read there: "For since nobody can be saved who has not first believed, it is the first task of the priest . . . to preach the Gospel of God to all men",[31] and the priests' ministration "begins with the announcement of the Gospel. . . ."[32] It has to be understood, of course, that such beginnings are not accomplished once and for all so as to be "completed" at a specific time; it rather never ends and demands continuous and always renewed efforts. And one more consideration has to be mentioned here. It has rightly been observed that "ordination as such does not yet confer everything necessary for living out fully the priestly office."[33] Nevertheless, this truth remains: the "sacred authority" to celebrate the Eucharist, *in persona Christi* and for the entire Church, is bestowed on the priest complete and unabridged in the very act of ordination itself, whether he is a learned man or not, experienced or not—this authority and another as well, to dispense absolution.

We should now deal with a *second* area of priestly

---

[31] *Decree on the Ministry and Life of Priests,* art. 4.

[32] *Decree on the Ministry and Life of Priests,* art. 2.

[33] *Publik,* Jan. 2, 1970, p. 23.

activity, subordinated to the first and secondary yet nonetheless authentically "priestly". This activity is aimed at leading people toward the Eucharist and preparing them for a mature participation in this sacrament of unity, love, and peace.[34] In addition to the celebration of the other sacraments (baptism, reconciliation, anointing) we should mention here above all every action that could be called "pastoral ministry", especially "proclamation" in the most comprehensive sense, all forms of teaching from religious instructions to public pronouncements in the mass media. "Social work", of course, may also be part of "pastoral ministry". It is difficult to understand the thinking of those who consider the priesthood to be a "part-time" occupation or even a "hobby",[35] not a full-time job. This is all the more strange for the fact that in this area, in contrast to the authority conferred in ordination, all important skills have to be acquired through the toil of personal experience. And this in turn seems hardly possible without the foundation of a genuine spirituality, which means the foundation of a contemplative style of life.

[34] *Scripta super libros, Sententiarum* 4 d. 24, 1, 3, 2 ad 1; *Summa contra Gentes* 4, 74.
[35] Illich, "Das Verschwinden des Priesters", 68, 71.

But is it at all possible to exclude from the realm of authentic priestly activity those at times outstanding contributions, say, to ethnology or to the linguistics of native tribes, achievements on the part of missionaries in view of a more effective proclamation of the Gospel? Hundreds of other examples could be listed. The decisive point in all such efforts is the aim that establishes a connection to the primary purpose of the priestly office. As should be expected, we find countless levels of intensity here, from the passionate integrating energy with which Teilhard de Chardin combined scientific research and priestly intention to lead man, in his own words, to the "greater Christ", up to that "double life", as it were, in which other and no less devout priests gained fame at the same time as outstanding ornithologists, formicologists, and historians. The theological auxiliary disciplines, such as the history of religion, New Testament exegesis, and perhaps even theology itself, are potentially both—authentic "priestly activity" and also occupations that simply happen to be engaged in by a priest. Every so often one might wonder whether the theologian whose attitude is not only unpriestly but also outright unbelieving may not perhaps be an especially crucial problem and danger for contemporary Christianity.

A similar situation, as everybody knows, is found regarding that multifaceted phenomenon whose name, "social work", already mentioned, is a vague generality rather than a definition. The German bishop Emmanuel von Ketteler voiced his protest against the social injustices of his time, in an entirely legitimate manner, through a series of sermons in the cathedral at Mainz. And hundreds after him, priests dedicated to social justice, advocates for the rights of the oppressed, have explicitly declared that humane living conditions are the necessary prerequisite for any meaningful participation at God's banquet table and have worked to that end. In the black ghetto of an American city I have met priests who, with admirable self-denial and remarkable success, were active as social workers to find solutions to the housing problems there. Yet in all this they refused to mention anything about Christ to their charges and were even less willing to speak of the sacrament of love and peace. This I shall never understand; still, who am I to judge! One thing, however, seems to me beyond doubt: such activity, although performed by priests, is nevertheless not a "priestly activity" in the strict sense. This applies with all the more reason to priests who decide to get involved in political revolutions, like some of them in South America, making headlines all over the world. And yet even Camillo Torres, the enthusiastically celebrated idol of the younger generation—by now almost forgotten—was well aware of the essentials and said so clearly. On the very day when he shed his priestly garb he declared publicly to be "chosen by Jesus Christ as priest for ever"[36] and that now he would renounce "the deeply cherished prerogative" to celebrate the sacrament of Christ's Body and Blood—which, once again, constitutes the inner essence of being a priest.

[36] German Guzman, *Camillo Torres: Persönlichkeit und Entscheidung* (Munich, 1970), 15, 146.

CHAPTER THREE

WHAT MAKES A BUILDING A CHURCH?

WHAT I AM ATTEMPTING here, to answer the title question, can in fact be only a preliminary consideration. Nevertheless, I wish to begin by emphatically stating my thesis: *a Christian church, in essence, is a sacred space.*

You do not have to be well versed in contemporary literature concerning church architecture in order to realize the vehemence with which this thesis is rejected by certain architects, even by some theologians. Not a few of them would probably refuse so much as to join in a serious discussion of it. Among the theses adopted at the well-publicized Conference on Church Architecture, sponsored by the Evangelical Academy in Bad Boll (February 1965), there explicitly appears the demand "to renounce the concept of the sacred".[1] And a Catholic theologian, a prolific writer on this subject, sums up his own thinking in these words: "Christian churches are not sacred spaces".[2] A collection of essays on the same topic declares in its title that our present time has moved

---

Text of an address to theologians and artists, June 2, 1970, in Münster. Printed in *Hochland* 63 (1971) and later published by Verlag der Arche (Zurich).

[1] *Kirchen für die Zukunft bauen* (Churches for the Future), ed. G. Rombold (Vienna, Freiburg, and Basel, 1969), 120 (hereafter *Zukunft*).

[2] *Christliche Kunstblätter*, no. 1 (1968).

"beyond the era of the sacred".[3] The "era of the sacred" would be over, a thing of the past; the task before us would be to build "churches for the future"—the title of another book published in 1969.[4]

Relevance, Progress, the Future

The demands to be relevant, progressive, and future oriented, advanced by this chorus of opposing voices, do indeed have a point. All the same, I wish to share with you the following three considerations, in form of a short digression, as it were.

First: "Relevance" is essentially an ambivalent concept. Relevant is not only what an era wants and likes but also those things that are simply needed (and that possibly are not quite appealing). Relevant may also be the rejection of contemporary fashionable positions; the corrective counterpoint to them certainly is. Nietzsche gave his polemical pamphlets against "a mere decorative culture", as he called it, the title *Unzeitgemässe Betrachtungen* (Untimely reflections). But he was

[3] *Kirchen in nachsakraler Zeit* (Church architecture after the era of the sacred), ed. H. E. Bahr (Hamburg, 1968) (hereafter *Nachsakral*).

[4] See n. 1 above.

convinced, and rightly so, that they were extremely "timely", extremely relevant. Should we, therefore, have indeed moved "beyond the era of the sacred" (whatever this means), then it may well be precisely the "sacred" that is relevant, even more relevant than ever before.

Second: Nobody can determine whether a specific action is "progressive" or not unless the inner significance of such action is acknowledged. In the early fifties the pedagogical discussions in the United States were dominated by the slogan of "progressive education". When I asked a colleague at a certain university what he meant by this, he answered, tongue in cheek, but not entirely: progressive is that school where the children learn only what they themselves like. As a matter of fact, such "progressivism" in many American schools has subsequently caused a serious erosion of the quality of education in mathematics and science, subjects generally not well liked. It took the shock of the *Sputnik* in October 1957 to drive home in one instant the truth that the inner reason for all learning is evidently to know the real world and its intrinsic laws. Therefore, the more a school system respects this inner reason, the more progressive and up to date it will be. What this means for our main topic is rather obvious. Whether a particular church architecture is "progressive" or not can be determined only after it is decided what a church is and what its purpose "should" be. Yet this is precisely the issue here, the core of the ongoing controversy.

Third: Regarding the demand to be "future oriented", it should suffice to ask: For what other reason have churches ever been built than "for the future"? It was always and inevitably an *unknown* future—as seen, for example, in the cathedral of Chartres, which now serves as a center for the international student pilgrimage, seven hundred years after the construction was completed!

These marginal comments, of course, do not yet support or explain in any way our main thesis that the edifice of a Christian church derives its identity from the "quality of the sacred".

An Unexpected Confirmation

It seems noteworthy to me that our thesis was recently confirmed in a way by none other than the opposing party. At first, this may come as a surprise, and it probably happened unwittingly but appears to be entirely logical. The source is a contemporary architect, a prize winner in numerous architectural competitions for church buildings. In his theoretical and programmatic statements (included in both collections of essays mentioned above) this architect opposes with exceptional intransigence any conception of the sacred. Commenting on his most recent church designs, he characterizes them as spaces "in which people may even dare to 'eat sausages' ".[5] This same essay, so my contention, contains a statement that not only confirms my position but also in effect repeats it. The statement in question reads thus: "To speak of a modern 'church' building as such should really no longer be possible."[6] I think here it is clearly stated that a building explicitly conceived as a nonsacred space is indeed not a church and should no longer be given that title. In order to express the very same thought in a positive formulation I may simply repeat what I said before: a Christian church, in essence, is a sacred space. Our thesis, standing against this contrasting background, may by now appear more pronounced, with sharper contours. Yet, clearly, supporting arguments are still wanting—if such arguments are possible at all! What "reasons" are there that would define what a church is and deter-

[5] *Zukunft*, 159.
[6] *Nachsakral*, 120.

mine which characteristics are essential? And above all: *Who* might claim legitimacy in advancing such a definition?

The "Sacred" Is Not an Aesthetic Category

A preliminary answer would be this: the architect, for one, may *not* claim such legitimacy! As a principle, neither the concept of "church" nor that of the "sacred" could as such be subsumed under categories of design and architecture, not even under the more general categories of art, style, and aesthetics. No, these concepts fall by right within the context of philosophical and theological anthropology. Consequently, the architect, as architect, would not be in a position to know what it is that makes a building a church. Whether he likes it or not, he will have to obtain this information from somewhere else. That in itself is not at all so unusual. Does he not have to seek information also about the functional requirements, say, of a school building (or a theater, a hospital, a bank)?

And yet, in the area of church architecture we witness an adverse and almost pathological sensitivity regarding any advice coming from the one agency that can claim a particular competence in this field. Thus we hear it proclaimed that the church architect's freedom concerning formal details, usually not questioned, "is no longer sufficient".[7] And we hear indignant protests against the perceived presumption "that church architecture would be studied in a school of theology instead of in a school of architecture".[8] A third voice attacks the "tyranny of the liturgy"[9] and demands that the "liturgy as primary norm" be replaced by imagination, by "utopia".[10] We may well assume that such angry gestures of self-defense are reactions to very concrete experiences. But I am convinced they are rooted in more fundamental general attitudes. I imagine the medical specifications for the construction of a hospital to be quite stringent and very detailed, yet never has anybody heard the ironic question whether from now on the architecture of a hospital might be studied in medical school.

Why this difference in reaction? The reason is, I think, that the construction of a hospital (or a school, or a theater) demands the advice of an expert whose judgment is more or less automati-

[7] *Nachsakral,* 120.
[8] *Nachsakral,* 52.
[9] *Nachsakral,* 81.
[10] *Nachsakral,* 92.

cally accepted. The edifice of a church, in contrast, is ostensibly *not* meant to serve a restricted specialized segment of life but man as such, in his total being. And so just about everybody, with some justification, has a real or at least imagined claim to be competent here.

All the same, there does exist in this world an authority entrusted, among other things, with the responsibility to proclaim and uphold precisely this challenge to man's totality, this call to an essential awareness so indispensable for a truly human existence. Whoever sets out to answer the further question, where this authority might be found and whether indeed it be real, cannot avoid revealing his innermost convictions. Otherwise he would already have resigned himself not to be able to say anything relevant concerning the construction of "churches".

When the Church Speaks "in Self-Expression"

To the inquiry, then, as to which authority may be entitled to define the concept of "church" and the essential qualities that make a building a church, I answer: *this authority is the Church when speaking "in self-expression"*.

I use the term *Church* in an entirely traditional understanding, by taking the literal meaning de-

rived from its Greek root, *kyriakē:* the historically conditioned actual existence of "the Lord's
[*Kyrios*] holy people"[11] —*in* the world, yet not
of the world.

The further question, however, as to when the
Church would be speaking "in self-expression"
does not have such a simple answer. During a
recent discussion the somewhat dejected comment
was made that in actual practice it may be just
the respective diocesan building commission that
acts as "the" Church. Such a comment would
be all the more appropriate when applied, for
instance, to the archbishop of Cologne, who
shortly before World War I decreed that all new
churches in his diocese must be constructed in
no other style than neoromanesque or neogothic.
Even more disturbing seems to me the disarm-
ingly naïve advice coming from the Swiss church
architect Hermann Baur, who exhorts architects
to keep "in close contact" with those modern
theologians who have reflected on the Church's
new function in society.[12] Looking for specifics,
more likely than not the architect may be told—
and I quote the theological editor of the collection
Churches for the Future—that "to build churches

[11] See K. Rahner and H. Vorgrimler, *Kleines theologisches
Wörterbuch* (Freiburg: Herder, 1961), 198.
[12] H. Baur, *Das Münster* 22 (1965): 361.

as 'sacred spaces' would be an attempt not only to impose on modern man an archaic religiosity" but also "to supplant the genuine Christian faith with a pre-Christian religiosity".[13]

Obviously, neither the latest theological jargon nor some personal episcopal preference constitutes the Church's formal "speaking as Church". When, indeed, does the Church speak "in self-expression"? Let me say, for example: in the official ritual of the consecration of a church and in the decrees of the Second Vatican Council.

When we, at this point, rather abruptly speak of the *Catholic* Church alone, we do not so much reveal an incidental preference or narrowness of this writer as rather a painful and complicated aspect of the subject matter itself—a point we shall have to consider further on.

The (Catholic) Church, then, speaking "as Church", not only *terms* a church a "sacred" building but also *makes* it into such by a specific liturgical rite. But what precisely *is* this sacred character? What does it mean?

Confusion of Terms

To attempt an answer here is all the more indispensable the more difficult it becomes to make

[13] *Zukunft*, 93.

oneself understood in the present Babel of confusing terms. Thus we hear that "sacred" would
mean "the emotional impact of a space"[14] and
more precisely an atmosphere marked by elements
of "archaicism" and "hierarchicism".[15] But above
all, the "sacred" would involve a sentimental air
and mysterious, emotionally charged theatrics.[16]
Another author maintains that the "sacred" stands
for symbols still employed in the liturgy but incomprehensible by now in an everyday setting.[17]
Still others connect the sacred essentially to concepts such as "arrogant pomp",[18] "undemocratic
aristocratism",[19] "triumphalistic and oppressive
architecture",[20] and so on. As can be seen, all
these labels, negative without exception, were advanced in recent years. I do not deny that such
labels, historically speaking, may indeed apply
in certain instances, though perhaps only in instances of aberration and corruption, which are
always more or less alluring possibilities. And
yet, all these characterizations have absolutely

---

[14] *Nachsakral*, 69.

[15] *Nachsakral*, 69.

[16] *Christliche Kunstblätter*, no. 1 (1968). *Zukunft*, 171.
Nachsakral, 117.

[17] *Zukunft*, 41.

[18] *Christliche Kunstblätter*, no. 1 (1968): 5.

[19] *Nachsakral*, 18.

[20] *Christliche Kunstblätter*, no. 1 (1968): 5. *Nachsakral*, 18.

nothing to do with the concept of the sacred as understood by the Church speaking "in self-expression". I deem it in fact necessary to explain the fundamental meaning of this term step by step and before all else.

Incidentally, the editor of *Church Architecture after the Era of the Sacred* opens his programmatical introduction by quoting four news reports: Bishop Helder Camara of Brazil petitions the city council to finance necessary apartment houses rather than a projected new church; in Ecuador, German Cardinal Döpfner is presented with a letter deploring the construction of a magnificent cathedral in the center of a slum area; citizen groups in Hamburg request funds for the "representative restoration" of churches in the city; and, in a village near Zagreb, Archbishop Seper consecrates a barn for the liturgy "after the Yugoslav authorities barred the use of a house that had been purchased for this purpose". As telling and touching as these four contemporary snapshots may be, the first three, nevertheless, do not contribute anything to a better understanding of our topic, which is the "sacred". The fourth instance, however, is all the more revealing, though perhaps not exactly in the sense the author had intended: the archbishop consecrates a barn for the liturgy.

"Consecratio" and "Aedes Sacra"

The Church since earliest times has unswervingly maintained precisely this: a building becomes a church not because of its architecture but through consecration. *Praestat ecclesias solemniter consecrari,* the "General Instruction" for the new Roman Missal, states,[21] "Needless to say, churches are to be solemnly consecrated"—even though the building be a barn. The *Pontificale Romanum* (in force until 1977), containing texts and rituals of blessings reserved for bishops, employs in its title for church dedications two different though almost synonymous terms: *De ecclesia dedicatione et consecratione. Dedicatio* means setting apart from the realm of commonly used objects. *Consecratio,* then, indicates the actual sanctification of an object thus set apart, its "transformation into a *res sacra*",[22] that is, into something sacred.

The consecration of a church, therefore, is something entirely different from, say, the solemn launching of a ship or the ribbon-cutting ceremony to "dedicate" a bridge, a highway, or a bowling alley. Such "dedications" have no other significance than "to open up for public use";

[21] No. 255.
[22] *Reallexikon für Antike und Christentum,* 3:643f.

they do not add anything substantial. It is precisely this aspect that makes all the difference compared to *consecratio*. This is even more evident when considering the terms used in biblical Greek to describe the dedication of the temple:[23] *enkainia, enkainizein*. *Kainos* means "new"; *enkainizein* means "to make new" (*innovare* in Latin).[24] A building, through consecration, is made into something it has not been before; it is transformed into a church, a sanctuary, an *aedes sacra*. This latter term, incidentally, is used consistently in official texts since Vatican II to denote a church building, although in the religious language of ancient Rome it already meant "a temple" (as the dictionaries attest). Some observers pointed out that this term was chosen deliberately to replace and supplant that other expression, "house of God", once commonly used and with much less hesitation. This is probably true. Nevertheless, I do not think that those biblical expressions—never intended, of course, to be strict definitions—have consequently lost their justification: *domus Dei, domus Domini, domus tua, locus habitationis tuae* (God's house, house of the Lord, thy house, thy dwelling place).

[23] I Kings 8:63; Jn 10:22.
[24] D. Stifenhofer, *Die Geschichte der Kirchweihe vom 1.–7. Jahrhundert* (Munich 1909), 18f.

By no means, indeed, are these vividly descriptive titles the only terms open to misconceptions and misinterpretations. The more abstract term *aedes sacra* (sacred space or sacred building) often enough causes some basic misunderstanding—on the part not only of "outsiders" but also of "insiders". If this title is taken as indicating a quality "substantially" inherent in the church edifice itself,[25] or if it is intimated, with Harvey Cox, that "the sacred space itself becomes the object of religious reverence" ("The earth is man's garden . . . but not an object of religious reverence", says he),[26] then the core of the matter is simply missed, and we are dealing with utter ignorance.

Not for *its own sake* is a church being consecrated, that is, made into an *aedes sacra,* a sacred space, a holy dwelling. Rather, the reason is to create a shelter, a repository for something that in a much more intensive and appropriate sense ought to be called—and kept—"sacred". The news report about the barn in Zagreb is entirely to the point: "consecreated *for the liturgy*"! But now, indeed, the question arises: What does "liturgy" mean, and why should it be considered "sacred" on a higher level?

Yet even before we consider this new question,

[25] *Nachsakral,* 10.
[26] *Nachsakral,* 99.

we are in a position to formulate rather precisely
the reason for calling a church a "sacred space".
It means, first, that a church, through a specific
act of consecration, has been set apart from the
realm of ordinary everyday life marked by considerations of work, wages, job security, usefulness,
consumption, and generally by the active pursuit
of practical purposes. Another way of expressing
this would be: set apart from the realm of the
"profane"—if only this term, in the contrasting
pair of "sacred" versus "profane", had not been
so extensively misconstrued by now with mythical, archaic, and magical elements that it has become almost hopeless to indicate anything precise
and reasonable with its use. The realm of the
profane belongs neither to the "devil"[27] nor to
"nothingness" nor to "darkness".[28] It simply
means the area outside the gates to the sanctuary,
the world of practical things, the marketplace,
the sports arena, the movie theater—all part, to
be sure, of the universal reality created by God
and entrusted to man: "He has made everything
beautiful in its time", as the Bible says (Sir 3:11).
Jesus' cleansing of the temple was most assuredly
not inspired by anticapitalism; it had nothing to

[27] *Zukunft*, 29, 80.
[28] *Nachsakral*, 11.

do with declaring money to be "of the devil". Jesus did not object to the exchange of currency, no more than he did to the sale of pigeons. All he said was: This is my Father's house and not a marketplace! On this point, however, he insists with absolute determination; he would not even allow anyone to carry utensils across the courtyard of the temple (Mk 11:16). Nobody, of course, objects to anyone's "eating sausages". But in view of the Lord's Supper Paul already cried out, "What! Do you not have houses to eat and drink in?" (1 Cor 11:22)—a word that classical theology has always taken to mean that God's house is reserved for sacred things; it is not a place for the ordinary daily activities of life.[29]

The consecrated enclosure, therefore, being "set apart", establishes explicit boundary lines between the area of the ordinary and everyday life "outside" and an "inside" where different norms of behavior obtain.

Incidentally, the same applies to the barn-made-church in Zagreb. To be sure, I have not seen it, but I am convinced that nobody would mistake it for a true barn any longer. Not only does it no longer shelter any animals, of course. But

[29] Thomas Aquinas, *Commentary on 1 Corinthians*, chap. 11, lect. 4.

should a Western tourist, for instance, enter there, even when no liturgy is taking place, he would behold the sacred symbols of Christianity; he would see the sanctuary light burning near the altar. There may be some people praying, on their knees, in silence. And not even a "starving" tourist would presume that this was a place for him "to eat sausages".

In short, this now is an *aedes sacra,* a sacred space specifically and explicitly set apart for the liturgy.

Liturgy and Altar

Once again, then: What is the meaning of "liturgy"? The most "progressive" article in the book *Church Architecture after the Era of the Sacred* contains a chapter entitled "Liturgy—Guided Meditation or Free Political Argumentation?"[30] My answer to this provocative question comes without hesitation and with complete confidence: neither the one nor the other! Neither one deserves to be called "liturgy", and neither requires a sacred space, a church. The same author, following out the logic of his position, states elsewhere[31] that "the discussion, so urgent in our days, has finally

[30] *Nachsakral,* 123.
[31] *Zukunft,* 153.

developed; it will have to face ever anew the question whether we should build churches at all, or rather something more needed and more appropriate."

Yet the question still remains as to the specific nature of "liturgy" that would claim a church as its proper place, and what it is that makes it "sacred" on a higher level. Since this question is complicated for several reasons, I wish to approach it in a roundabout way. This has the advantage, however, of leading inevitably to one of the decisive elements of church design and church architecture: the altar. The statement that the altar is "of decisive importance" in church architecture begs, of course, the preliminary question: What indeed *is* an altar?

This is the crucial question. Above all, it brings out the real and fundamental differences between the Christian denominations, which *no amount* of ecumenical goodwill alone is able to eliminate. Consider the following statements: the edifice of the church is "nothing else but . . . a place of shelter surrounding the altar on which the mystery of the Incarnation is centered". And further: "Churches and cathedrals have been erected to surround not a book but the altar." These sentences were uttered by a famous contemporary Protestant theologian, Walter Uhsadel, who also maintains that Martin Luther himself still "consid-

ered the Mass, the sacramental liturgy centered
on the altar, to be the first and preeminent liturgy
of the assembly".[32] And yet these remarks, while
expressing Catholic teaching quite accurately, can
hardly be taken as typical of Protestant thinking.
Catholic conception indeed attributes to the altar
a greater importance than to the church building
as such. There is no rite of church dedication
without the solemn consecration of the altar as
its necessary core,[33] while an altar can very well
receive consecration by itself and apart from its
surrounding church building.[34] The liturgical
norms concerning the design of the altar, even
in as recent a document as the "General Instruction" of 1969, are unusually detailed and strict.
For instance, the altar should not only be firmly
attached to the floor but also, as a rule, should
be of natural stone because, it is emphasized, of
its "symbolic significance".[35] All this, quite obviously, may appear strange and odd to anybody

[32] W. Uhsadel, "Der Altar ist keine Kulisse", *Zeitwende*
(1966): 519.

[33] *Institutio Generalis,* nos. 262, 265.

[34] Thomas Aquinas, *Summa theologica* 3, 83, 3 ad 2.

[35] *Institutio Generalis,* no. 263. See also *Summa theologica*
3, 83, 3 ad 5. Visiting the United States recently, I noticed
that the official translation of the *Institutio Generalis* simply
omits this expression (*iuxta . . . significationem*)!

who is not aware of what happens on the altar according to the Church's belief—the Catholic Church's belief, that is.

What happens there, in the words of the Second Vatican Council, is the celebration of the Eucharistic mystery and thus the actualization of the unique sacrifice of Christ himself,[36] who is in truth and fact present under the signs of bread and wine and who unites himself with the brethren gathered in faithful celebration.[37] I realize full well that these claims will sound utterly peculiar, simply unbelievable, to ears attuned to commonsense and down-to-earth discourse. I myself would not accept them, not even from the most distinguished theologian, were their truth not assured by "God's own word". But this is not the point here. The point here, first and foremost, is the significance of the altar within the context of church architecture, in consequence of the underlying conviction. This means: the altar is *not* a mere piece of furniture, *not* a mere depository for books and utensils; it is not at all "a table like any other table found, let us say, in the confirmation classroom" (as one Protestant church architect puts it).[38] Rather, the

---

[36] *Dogmatic Constitution on the Church,* art. 28.

[37] *Constitution on the Sacred Liturgy,* art. 7.

[38] *Nachsakral,* 62.

spiritual symbolism centered on the altar makes it a twofold reality: the altar, on the one hand, serves as *table* for the ritual meal, and on the other, constitutes a "stone of sacrifice"[39] (*la pierre du sacrifice*).[40] Under the frequent name *lapis iste,* this stone is the altar explicitly seen, in the official rite of consecration and also in classical theology, as related to the biblical altars of sacrifice erected by the likes of Abel, Abraham, Isaac, Jacob, and Moses but also and above all as related to the Rock that is Christ,[41] the one and only Sacrifice, and to the altar of the Cross.[42] This is no reason, however, to call the altar "a sacred monument", as does, sardonically, one of our Catholic theologians.[43] But there is even less reason to reduce the altar to a mere symbol of something like fellowship around the dinner table, no matter how motivated and ennobled by religious considerations such fellowship may be.

[39] T. Filthaut, in A. Henze, *Kirchliche Kunst der Gegenwart* (Recklinghausen, 1954), 42.

[40] J. Gélineau, "L'église, lieu de la célébration", *La Maison-Dieu* 63 (1960): 45.

[41] *Summa theologica* 3, 83, 3 ad 5.

[42] *Summa theologica* 3, 83, 1 ad 2.

[43] *Zukunft,* 105; cf. also Goergen and Gatz, in Weyres and Barting, *Kirchen* (Munich 1959), 24.

Celebrating the Sacred Mysteries

What we have said here also bears on our question as to the nature of the "liturgy", for the sake of which an altar and a sacred space are appropriate and required in the first place. This, then, secondly, has transpired: "liturgy" in its primary sense does not mean a symbolic common meal or an assembly merely for instructions in the Faith, for "communal meditation on God's will in relation to our neighbor",[44] for human interaction among those "who speak the needed word to each other",[45] least of all for the triggering of a social process that "explicitly remains within the context of public and political discourse".[46] "Liturgy," rather, means in essence the celebration of sacred mysteries, *actio sacra praecellenter*,[47] "a sacred action surpassing all others". What the proclamation of the word, at its best, only announces, and what all human cultures have somehow foreknown, yearned for, and often enough prefigured—it becomes *reality* in this sacred

[44] *Nachsakral,* 109.
[45] *Nachsakral,* 108.
[46] *Nachsakral,* 126.
[47] *Constitution on the Sacred Liturgy,* art. 7.

action: the true presence of God among men.

This is a reality that stands outside the normal process of human existence and absolutely outside the occurrences of everyday life. And it is *this* reality that by its intrinsic nature requires the sheltering space explicitly set apart, in its turn, from the ordinary framework of daily chores, the protecting boundary, the sacred precinct, the *aedes sacra*.

To be sure, preaching and fraternal meal, conversation and reflective response to the challenge of daily life "outside", all these are included in a Christian liturgy. And yet, I consider it of fundamental importance to hold fast to the distinction between the *actio sacra* proper, the celebration of the sacred mystery, and the proclamation and interpretation of God's truth. This distinction has immediate relevance in view of church architecture; I maintain it to be one of the *praeambula* (premises) whose acceptance or rejection will be much more consequential than may appear at first. Proclamation, instruction, teaching, preaching, information—all these, by their very nature, are not confined to the "inside" but are also and especially intended for the "outside", in view of the realm of everyday existence where people ordinarily spend most of their lives. It is for this good reason, to reach people where they are, that Christian proclamation uses all available means and techniques of communication. And it is only logical for those who hold such proclamation to be the essence of the Christian liturgy that they cannot see why a separate sacred precinct should be required for *that*. The medieval lawbook of Gratian the monk, who in turn quotes a very early synod, already establishes that neither pagans nor Jews nor heretics should be prevented from entering the Christian church and listening to the word of God—but only during the "Mass of the catechumens",[48] that is, not after the actual celebration of the sacred mystery has begun. To this celebration, indeed, not even those are admitted who prepare for baptism. The sacred mystery itself, according to its inner nature, is celebrated only by those who have been initiated and who profess their faith in adoration. They are gathered in an "inner sanctum" set apart from the "outside", be it even that the separating wall is formed by only the living bodies of the participants themselves, as has happened often enough in the concentration camps and prisons of totalitarian regimes.

If this distinction between the celebration of

[48] *Corpus Juris Canonici* 3: *De consecratione*, dist. 1, cap. 67; see also *Summa theologica* 3, 83, 4 ad 4.

the "sacred mysteries" and the "proclamation of the word" is denied or watered down, as seems to be almost the rule nowadays, then there will appear, not at all surprisingly, two dangerous consequences, both of them, I maintain, equally acute at present: either the risk of a demonstrative informality and familiarity in speech and comportment, devastating to the character of the "sacred action"; or the risk of an aberrant idolizing of the "word," whose architectural "enclosure" can indeed produce—as one Protestant theologian puts it—only an "ostentatious and embarrassing 'sacred' air".[49]

Making the Sacred Tangible

In this concluding section I intend to venture a tiny step beyond the realm of the *praeambula,* the premises. In doing so, I have to admit that my reflections so far leave open almost all concrete possibilities in church architecture. To put it less kindly: they are, on a practical level, quite useless. In particular, they hardly contribute to the solution of certain sociological difficulties, which the contemporary church architect also has to consider: church location in a purely residential area, business districts depopulated on Sundays, prob-

[49] *Nachsakral,* 22.

lems in the suburbs, and so on. Nothing was said on all this, but then, I did not set out to do so anyway.

All the same, the question is justified whether this basically invisible quality of the sacred could and should be made tangible in a particular form of architecture, and if so, *how*. It has been observed—in very apt terms, in my opinion—that the true locus of God's real presence is indeed the worshiping assembly itself, so that the purpose of any church, existing or to be constructed, is nothing else but "to provide the surrounding space for this living presence".[50] If this is so, then we should be curious as to the translation of such a conceptual purpose into visible architectural design and what a "religious" building of this kind should appropriately look like. But does not this immediately return the entire controversy, put aside here on purpose, regarding the "emotional impact" of a structure, its pomposity, its triumphalism, and so on?

Let me respond first with some negative specifications, that is, with the attempt to say, in opposition to certain contemporary claims, what a church building definitely is *not,* and what it should *not* look like.

[50] Goergen and Gatz, 20.

If a church architect, for instance, declares that in his thinking "a church building" is as much a "commodity"[51] as a newspaper, then all further discussion with him, I think, becomes pointless. A sacred space is exactly the opposite of a "commodity". Just so could the *actio sacra,* the sacrificial offering, be defined as the opposite of a "useful" and "profitable" action. This truth, of course, has to become visibly apparent in some manner. Thus the church building is not simply "another sector of our own dwellings", to use the words found in the first of several "demands" that have been advanced to provide "new impulses to church architecture".[52] Nor are terms such as "comfortable", "intimate", *habitabilité*[53] adequate concepts to judge the authenticity of a church building.

We also hear the further demands that modern church structures should be integrated into their extended surroundings more than before, and that their exteriors should show barely any distinguishing characteristics (*un minimum de différenciation extérieure*).[54] It is, of course, all important

[51] *Zukunft,* 135.

[52] *Zukunft,* 173.

[53] D. F. Debuyst, *Architecture Moderne et Célébration Chrétienne* (Bruges, 1966), 41; D. F. Debuyst, in *Christliche Kunstblätter,* no. 1 (1968): 18.

[54] Debuyst, *Architecture,* 20.

here what the terms *integration* and *differentiation* actually mean. But in a general way and with equal justification we might argue that it is inherent to the reality considered here to be "different" and "nonintegrated". And we should not hesitate to challenge contemporary man with the needed experience of this "difference", which means that such difference must be made tangible.

Just suppose, as a perfect analogy, that some people would want poetry to use only "rational", ordinary, even trivial everyday language—which, indeed, is actually happening—so that the lyric vocabulary, thus "banned", can now be mercifully adopted by cigarette commercials. Or suppose that philosophy would be expected—and this, too, is in fact happening—to abandon those insoluble topics such as the meaning of death, the *commentatio mortis,* to "integrate" itself into the field of scientific research, and to produce verifiable and above all useful results like any exact science. All this would not only impoverish our existence but also render it, basically, inhuman.

But as already mentioned, the demand to "integrate" the church building into the respective city environment can in actual fact mean many things. Take New York, for instance. Wandering through the canyons of her avenues, you may suddenly notice a church portal embedded in the mile-long walls of stone and concrete, and this may seem like perfect "integration". But upon entering you find yourself in a large hall, three or four stories high, the ceiling supported by columns. Confronted with this totally "different" environment, you experience a feeling of awe and, at the same time, of immense relief.

If "sacred" is to mean explicitly set apart from the realm of ordinary use and dedicated to the *cultus divinus,* then such "being different" becomes indeed decisive. Applied to the practical architectural design and expressed in positive terms, this implies two requirements only: first, a simple sheltering element, a separating wall, a *boundary* line, perhaps emphasized by a lobby and a courtyard, shutting out the hustle and bustle of the ordinary workday; and second, the *exclusive* reservation of the structure, at least in principle, for purposes of worship (the provision "in principle" is to mean that any nonliturgical usage should not be an explicit part of the architectural conception).

I firmly hold that such a construction of "sacred spaces" becomes all the more existentially indispensable, the more mere considerations of practical usefulness threaten to gain absolute dominance over the entire realm of human life. And all the more for the sake of a truly human existence does man stand in need of this opportunity to escape, every now and then, from that constant acoustical and visual noise, that continual vying for attention ("buy this, drink that, eat this, vote for me, get your fun here, demonstrate for this, protest against that")—escape, indeed, into a space where silence rules and true listening becomes possible, the awareness of *that* kind of reality by which our existence is sustained and ever again renewed and nourished.

These, then, are in my estimation the essential premises that church architecture has to satisfy, especially in our time. For the rest, there are no limits to the architect's creative invention. We should resist those apodictic demands that declare what a modern church building *must not* be and *must not* do, such as: "Our churches, beginning with their exteriors, must not appear imposing in any way",[55] or: "It is hypocrisy to design churches as conspicuous structures dominating their urban environment."[56] Here we touch on an aspect that we can mention only in passing: the "sacred space", by its very nature, does not derive its identity merely from its functional de-

[55] *Zukunft*, 206.
[56] *Zukunft*, 207. Similarly H. Baur, in *Das Münster* 22 (1969): 361.

sign like any other useful building; rather, and
beyond that, it must seek visible expression by
becoming itself sign and *symbol*.

The underlying invisible reality that seeks such
visible expression, however, can assume *many*
faces. The "Lord", from whom the assembly as
well as the building derive the name "Church",
is indeed the one persecuted and shamefully murdered, but he is *equally* the triumphant victor over
death. He is the servant of all, but also the "King
of kings and Lord of lords" (1 Tim 6:15). And
his fellowship is composed of "strangers and pil-
grims" (1 Pet 2:11) but also of "heirs to the Kingdom" (James 2:5). Thus the possibilities of
expressing this reality in a visible structure range,
indeed, from the barn in Zagreb—most certainly
recognizable as a church, even if it were only
through a secret sign such as the symbolic fish—
all the way to the cathedral that stands for the
heavenly Jerusalem.

All will agree, of course, that in our own time
neither the one nor the other conception would
in fact be viable options. We should, therefore,
talk in more specific terms. The awareness of
the "sacred" leaves room for utter exterior simplicity that even admits in certain instances the
barn of Zagreb as a legitimate possibility. But it
would exclude, on the other hand, that paltry

skimpiness wrongfully equated with poverty in the spirit of the Gospel, which in reality is nothing but lack of interest on the part of a secularized society.[57] And yet, there is also room for splendor and lavishness, which once again would include one thing and exclude another: excluded is the ostentatious display of wealth and worldly power; included, however, has to be the option to sacrifice for "God's house", as a token of joy and love, even the most treasured possession.

And as regards the possibility of a church building dominating the cityscape, it is an error flowing from a narrow sociological thinking to assume that such dominance would by necessity and primarily reflect any social or political claims on the part of the Church or even the denominational powers prevailing in a place.[58] It is an error not to consider that there may be manifested the faith in Christ's royal dominion or the conviction that the celebration of these mysteries occurs essentially as a public action in the midst of the world and with all of creation the backdrop, even though the actual place be a prison cell or the catacombs.

---

[57] See the report by H. Muck on a Swedish makeshift church in *Zukunft*, 111.

[58] *Zukunft*, 207.

To Be "Contemporary"

The common discourse on "modern" church architecture, it seems to me, regularly uses the notion of what is "contemporary" in too narrow a sense. Those who explicitly insist on being "of today" should indeed expect that tomorrow they will be considered "of yesterday". The Christian immersed in the life rhythm of the Church claims much larger dimensions for his "today", in geographical space as well as historical time. I think of the Requiem Mass for my brother inside the rotunda of St. Michael's in Fulda, a church dating back eleven hundred years. I think of the High Mass in Notre Dame on the feast of Corpus Christi, when the sequence *Lauda Sion* made me suddenly aware that a professor at the Paris university, Thomas Aquinas, had composed these lines seven hundred years earlier, and that he might have listened to its first recital in this very same cathedral. And I think of a Mass in 1963, inside the church built by one of Antonio Gaudi's students in memory of the martyrs of Nagasaki, a building rich in visual symbolism, with steeples reaching like two bare arms into the same sky out of which had fallen, in 1945, the atomic bomb. All this, undoubtedly, belongs to my own "today": the Gregorian chant, the traditional words, *and also the church buildings!* What is the unifying principle here, tying together all these thoroughly different buildings, bridging distances of a thousand years, and making them truly "contemporary"? It is alone the fact that every one of these buildings, right from the beginning, had been conceived and erected as shelter for the one and ever identical "sacred action" that makes such a building, in name and in fact, an *aedes sacra,* a sacred space.

What, then, is a "modern" church building, contemporary today and in the future? It is probably impossible to provide a theoretical definition of it. If perceived as a challenge, then such challenge is definitely not directed toward theoretical speculation but rather toward architectural creativity that can manifest itself and prove its validity as well only in the actual construction of a church building.

The question as to the degree of "freedom" here for the arts and the artist was answered by the Second Vatican Council,[59] and this answer imposes only one condition: that the sacred character of the consecrated space and the liturgical

[59] *Constitution on the Sacred Liturgy,* art. 123.

action it shelters be respected and safeguarded.

I wonder whether this can be called a "condition" at all. For it merely asks that the building to be constructed be truly a church.

CHAPTER FOUR

NO MERE WORDS BUT REALITY

The Sacrament of the Bread

NOT LONG AGO, a young city priest was featured on television at some length and showered with high praise. Instead of celebrating regular Sunday services, he would offhandedly meet with his youthful flock in their own hangout over pop and French fries. "Since you do not come and listen to my sermon, why should I not visit with you here, sit at your table, and talk with you?"

At first, this seems to make sense as the right thing to do. It remains unclear, though, whether this determined man thought such a conversation would accomplish the full purpose of the Christian liturgy, and if not its full purpose, then at least its more important aspect, its center. The producers of the television program mentioned were evidently of this opinion.

Be this as it may. The priest here, of course, is right in *one* respect. He simply follows the ancient insight that he who wants to teach must first go and find his audience, his listeners, wherever in fact they are, whether he likes those places or not: be it a discotheque, a beer joint around

A radio talk broadcast by Westdeutscher Rundfunk, March 1975, upon an invitation to respond to a theologian's lecture on the same topic, a lecture that this author had attacked as blasphemous.

the corner, a sidewalk in the city, or the easy chair in front of the television screen.

This commonsense rule had already guided Socrates in the marketplace of Athens in the same way, incidentally, as it guided the Apostle Paul several centuries later. If the Christian Faith, indeed, comes through hearing, then the first task will consist in speaking to someone who listens. After all, the Gospel is "Good News", a "joyful message". And a messenger is not someone who waits for others to come to him; instead, he himself goes out and searches for his audience.

The beginning, therefore, is always the *proclamation*. Christianity has at times neglected this obvious truth; or else, every now and then it has elevated it to an almost mystical level, blowing it up out of all proportion and making it the pinnacle of all wisdom. The Second Vatican Council, a few years ago, made this truth its own, putting it, however, in the proper perspective.

It is also quite evident that proclamation can indeed happen in any place at all. By necessity it has to take place wherever those to whom the message is addressed are found. And there is, of course, no reason at all why any of the available means of communication should not be employed for this purpose.

But here we should consider also the other side

of the coin. The spoken word and the proclamation do indeed constitute a beginning, but such a beginning has to be accomplished ever anew. And yet, the spoken word in itself is not central here. All speech by its very nature refers to something that is not speech. What is it? It is reality! In this context I am reminded of a saying a friend of mine is wont to repeat over and over, pointedly and like a refrain—and I myself agree with it entirely: I attend Church, not because of all the talking and preaching but because something happens there. Any one person's opinion, a friend's or one's own individual and private opinion, is admittedly of little consequence in matters of such importance. Relevant here, I think, is only what the Church herself, the *kyriakē* (which means the assembly consecrated to the Lord), has throughout the centuries believed and thought and professed about it. And the Church, too, declares the center of her liturgy to be indeed an action, something that "happens".

What, then, is happening there? The answer to this very question—an answer, it should be noted, given by the Church herself—shall be set forth here in the simplest terms possible, although I am a layman, not a priest or a theologian. Yes, it seems that nowadays *all* fundamental realities stand in need of the most elementary explanation and have to be proclaimed in the simplest terms.

Incidentally, I shall speak as a believer, as a Christian and a Catholic. And I presume that only another believer will agree with me. But I think also a nonbeliever can be expected at least to take notice of how a believer conceives these matters, as I would without doubt be interested to learn, say, how an orthodox Hindu sees and interprets the basic teachings of Hinduism.

First and foremost, and so as not to start out on the wrong track, one has to understand *this* about the central Christian liturgy: it is characterized by being derivative, subordinated, and secondary. What takes place in it is essentially an echo, a continuation of something other. More to the point, in a very precise sense (to be elaborated further on) it makes present and actualizes anew an event of the distant past, an event usually summed up in the theological concept of "Incarnation". This means that if this original event, an event that is first and primary not only in time but also in essence, is not accepted as truly having taken place, then any genuine grasping of what "happens" in the Church's liturgy, be it through mental acceptance or in active participation, becomes impossible.

This primordial event took place, as Scripture puts it, "in the fullness of time", which makes it, indeed, the central event of mankind's history. Truly, this event is not only difficult to grasp; much more, it is outright unbelievable, something I would not accept even from the most trustworthy journalist and the most profound philosopher or theologian—were it not authenticated by a *theios logos* (to use Plato's expression), a divine utterance, and thus by revelation in the strictest sense. We are dealing here with something utterly impossible—at least so it appears to our way of thinking. And yet, in the heart of our heart we know that all perfection, all fulfillment, all completeness seems to us *forever* impossible and unattainable. "Unreal to us the rose appears", declared Goethe in one of his poems. Evidently, I am talking just like the layman I am; the unfolding blossom of the rose, of course, represents a mystery infinitely inferior to the radiance of the event we are discussing here, an event that utterly transcends all human imagination: God himself becomes man, and—in the New Testament language of nomadic shepherds—"pitches his tent among us".

A circle comes to completion here; beginning and end, the very dawn of creation and the final act of the creative process, touch each other. And yet, as thus a ring is rounded, the whole of the story still remains untold. Looking only this far, our thinking—always aiming at some smooth "system"—would indeed be led down the wrong path of misinterpreting God's Incarnation in un-historic, gnostic terms.

For the core of this matter is such that it necessarily transcends any unifying universal "system". The core of this matter, indeed, consists in this: God becomes man in Jesus Christ and, in an act of self-sacrifice, at a historically determined date, "under Pontius Pilate", allows himself to be murdered by man, by his own people, so that we may share in God's own life.

We shall never understand why such a cruel sacrifice on that shameful tree should have been necessary—even though in the innermost recesses of our heart, really, we quite know that no one has a greater love than he who lays down his life for those he loves.

To repeat it: those who—for whatever reason—do not accept this primary event, God's Incarnation and Christ's self-sacrifice, as historical reality, will by necessity be unable to find any personal access to an understanding of the mystery celebrated in the Christian liturgy. As mentioned already, what "happens" in the Church's liturgy is derived from that primary event and thus is something secondary.

Incidentally, this formulation is easily misunderstood. It does not mean to say, for example and above all, that the Christian celebration would merely be some sort of commemoration by which the memory of things past is kept alive and present, though this would certainly be logical and meaningful.

At this point we should say a word in favor of a certain argument, advanced time and again by the mainstream of philosophical rationalism in the eighteenth and nineteenth centuries and aimed against Christianity. This argument, indeed, is basically quite mistaken, and yet it has some merit that deserves consideration. I am referring to the objection formulated in various terms by Kant, Lessing, and quite a few others, even up to our own time: Why should anybody be obligated, or at all be justified, to center his entire life on some historical event of the past? If it were a faith based on absolute and necessary truth—indeed, there would be no problem with that! But a "historical faith" (as Kant puts it) that refers us back to some event in the far-distant past, an event necessarily colored by many accidental circumstances: Can such a faith withstand the critique of reason?

Many things should be considered in this regard, not least the challenging question whether or not absolute and necessary truth would in any event be possible for only an equally absolute mind. And yet, *one* aspect of this objection is justified and to the point: if the divine Logos in fact has become man in Christ and has revealed itself, then such an event can never be conceived as limited merely to those few years at the beginning of our present calendar, almost twenty centuries ago. God's Incarnation—if it really happened, and if it indeed should confront a man to change his life—must necessarily be conceived as an event of abiding presence, now and for all future time—this, however, not in the form of a "necessary truth of reason", as Lessing postulated, but rather as a tangible historical event, incomprehensible, and grasped through faith alone, yet entirely real nevertheless.

Indeed, it is precisely this tangible presence of Incarnation and immolation that constitutes the very essence of the mystery celebrated in the Christian liturgy. It is this presence that the participant experiences as reality.

All fine and good, one may say here, but everything that happens visibly in the liturgical celebration possesses nevertheless an ultimately only symbolic quality. No, I would reply, what we have here is not "merely" a *symbol* but a *sacrament!* A sacrament, although belonging to the category of sign and symbol, is nevertheless not something "merely" symbolic. It not only signifies a certain reality, but its sign—and this is indeed unique— at the same time *effects* what it signifies, which means that it brings about an objective, enduring reality. Of course, this does not happen simply through some silent, "magic" ritual; the spoken word is not without importance, and words *are* being spoken. And yet, it appears highly questionable and above all easily misleading when a famous contemporary theologian declares the essence of a sacrament to consist in the spoken word. Not so! What sets the sacramental word apart and makes it unique is the fact that while it is uttered the reality it names comes about!

In the celebration of the liturgical mystery there occurs something that all forms of mankind's worship have desired and anticipated and have often enough also prefigured, namely, the true presence of God among men; more specifically: the real presence, within the celebrating community, of the incarnate divine Logos and his immolation. But it is the "celebrating" community! This fact clearly excludes the acceptance of just *any* place or *any* behavior. Realities of such dignity and loftiness simply cannot be celebrated in just *any* place or before some accidental gathering of indifferent people. Proceedings of this kind demand a space explicitly separated from the trivialities of every day. The separating wall may even be formed by the very bodies of the participants themselves, as has happened often enough in the concentration camps of various dictatorships. Essential above all is the presence of such a community that worships in faith.

Ordinarily (excepting extraordinary situations, which are not considered here) an *altar* is required as well. "Sacrament of the Altar"—this is *the* name for the central Christian mystery since pre-Augustinian times. But an altar, in its inner and spiritual meaning, is not merely a table, a piece of furniture; rather, it is at the same time the "stone of sacrifice" on which an offering is placed. This does not change the fact that the Christian altar, as the "table of the Lord", is essentially also the center of the sacred communal meal.

And this confronts us with one other aspect of our topic, with the question, namely, how can the Christian believer gain his promised and apportioned share in the reality that "happens" at this celebration, in the objective and tangible reality beyond all human words, beyond all proclamation and prayer, and underlying the symbolic action?

How do I become a participant? How can I be part of an actual event? My presence alone would evidently not be sufficient! Can mere watching ever be enough, even the most attentive and intensive watching? How, in this very special and entirely exceptional case, does "communication" happen, fashionable though this expression may sound? Incidentally, this term is not really distinct from the terms *communion* and *communicate,* terms that in Christian usage clearly and almost exclusively have always meant the specific participation and involvement discussed here. "To communicate"—this expression, indeed, has by now migrated from at first strictly sociological confines into the everyday language of the common man, thereby undergoing a certain generalization and dilution. Such "migrations" of meaning, of course, offer distinct opportunities for clarification; for it may at times be beneficial, even necessary, to single out something that has become all too familiar and to look at it with the eyes of the outsider, the uninitiated, and thus to discover the original meaning anew, unencumbered, and as if for the first time.

Such was my experience when I read that remarkable book *God Is Alive; I Met Him* by the French journalist André Frossard. This book, as is well known, had been for some time on the list of international best-sellers—which almost prevented me from paying any attention to it. In truth, what we have here is an impressive report by an otherwise quite "regular" modern secularist intellectual, a report that is unpretentious and simple and because of this so convincing. It tells of an experience that could well be called "mystical". The author, above all, describes his reactions to the ensuing and quite systematic discovery of Catholic Christianity and its teachings. With constantly renewed approval, Frossard says, he came to know the Church's teachings that up to then were no more than hearsay for him. One after the other of these teachings seemed to him right on target—except one! One point, he says, came entirely as a surprise and left him in utter astonishment, an astonishment in admiration, though: none other than the subject we are discussing here, man's participation in the divinity made present in the sacrament.

"That God's love would invent this unique way of communicating itself through the sign of bread, the fare of the poor! Of all the gifts of Christianity displayed in front of me, this was the most beautiful." So writes Frossard.

We now return to our initial question. The decisive and essential substance of what "happens" in the celebration of the Christian mystery is not any speech, any sermon. It is that dynamic reality of which the proclamation of the word, at best, gives a commentary: it is, indeed, the renewed actualization of Christ's sacrifice, a "happening" entirely beyond the regular course of everyday life and absolutely unique. And Christ, as his real and tangible presence in the sacred bread has now come about, becomes one with those who partake of this meal in faith and devotion.

Those, above all, whose reasoning moves mainly on an abstract and conceptual level—yes, especially those—find themselves, I might say, in danger of some kind of spiritual arrogance, looking at the utter directness of such communion with God himself as something all too physical and even primitive. In fact, when I was a student, I heard a certain professor of sociology call the sacred meal of Christianity a "tribal atavism". Even so great a thinker as Saint Augustine apparently had to fend off his own mental challenge when he insists, quite emphatically, that here we are *in no wise* dealing with a mere *verbal event* ("not the spoken word, not the written letter, not the resounding voice"), but with the *Body of the Lord,* made present in the material reality of earthly gifts.

What would appear as perhaps problematical and not spiritual enough to those sitting unperturbed at their desks has, in fact, shown itself ever anew to be a truly comforting and healing reality, indeed, the only enduring and supporting reality, to countless people in the extremes of their existence: to the prisoners of totalitarian regimes, to those facing certain death, to those in their final agony, who were no longer looking for any human encouragement, any spoken words, any sermons, but for the very reality of God—in the sacrament of bread.